CONTEMPORARY'S

Reading
Basics

D1516608

Advanced Reader

**McGraw-Hill
Contemporary**

ISBN: 0-8092-0669-2

Published by McGraw-Hill/Contemporary,
4255 West Touhy Avenue,
Lincolnwood (Chicago), Illinois 60712-1975 U.S.A.
© 2001 McGraw-Hill/Contemporary

123456789 VH 16 15 14 13 12 11 10 987654321

Table of Contents

To the Reader

If reading has never been easy for you, Contemporary's *Reading Basics* will help. Each selection in this reader will let you practice reading. The article or story will grab your interest and keep you reading to the end. When you finish reading, you will answer questions to

- check your understanding of the story
- apply reading skills to help your understanding of the story

You may answer these questions alone or with your classmates. You might write the answers or you might use the questions to have a discussion. Suggested answers to the questions are in the back of this book.

Your teacher may ask you to read a selection after a lesson in the workbook that ends with a Read On note. Or you may read these selections any time you wish. The final story, "Strange Case of Dr. Jekyll and Mr. Hyde" by Robert Louis Stevenson, has been included for extra reading practice or for listening while your teacher reads the story to you.

Reading Basics will build your confidence in your ability to read by letting you practice on short, interesting stories.

America's Natural Wonders

Which of America's national parks has some of the oldest and tallest trees in the world?

1 When you think of national parks, most likely you think of mountains and lakes. But our national parks include other natural wonders. There are beaches, deserts, caves, and forests. North, south, east, and west—our national parks are located all over the continental United States. You can also find them in Alaska, Hawaii, and the Virgin Islands.

History

2 The U.S. national park system began in 1872. That's when Congress passed a law making Yellowstone our first national park. Others were soon added. Yosemite [yoh•seh´•mih•tee], Sequoia [seh•kwoy´•ah], and Mount Rainier [ruh•neer´] were some of the earliest.

3 The National Park Service was formed in 1916. Its job is not only to care for national parks. It is also in charge of hundreds of historic sites. These include the Statue of Liberty and Ellis Island, Independence Hall in

Philadelphia, the Freedom Trail in Boston, and the Vietnam Veterans Memorial in Washington, D.C.

A Look at Some Parks

4 Here is a sampling of some scenic national parks. Perhaps you'll make time to visit them some day.

5 **The Carlsbad Caverns National Park** in New Mexico is unique. Here, you can see some of the world's largest caves. One of them, called the Big Room, is 285 feet high. It has a floor space the size of 14 football fields! Park visitors walk through underground passages to reach the caves. The ceilings, floors, and walls are covered with icicle-like shapes. They are stalactites, stalagmites, and crystals. These spires have taken thousands of years to form. In some cases, stalactites and stalagmites are joined, forming huge columns and pillars. Some of the shapes have names, such as King's Palace and Totem Pole. Besides these incredible formations, on summer nights, visitors can watch thousands of bats fly out of a part of the cavern called the Bat Cave.

6 **The Grand Canyon** in Arizona is one of the greatest natural wonders of the world. Over many centuries, the Colorado River wore down rock to create the canyon. It's about 1 mile deep, 18 miles wide, and 217 miles long. The kinds of land areas from top to bottom range from deserts to pine forests. Roads run along the North Rim and the South Rim, each with endless scenic views. Visitors can take pictures of special sights by tour bus. Many just want to enjoy the changing colors of the rocks as the sun moves across the canyon. People who want to explore the park further can take a mule ride into the canyon. Others can see the canyon in a thrilling raft ride down the Colorado River.

7 **Glacier National Park** is located in northwest Montana, close to Canada's border. The park has more than 200 lakes and 50 glaciers. Glaciers result from

changes in Earth over millions of years. Visitors can see them from their cars. Or they can let a park ranger take them for a closer look on foot or on horseback. One special highway in this park has been named Going-to-the-Sun Road. At almost every turn, visitors see snow-peaked mountains and shiny lakes and waterfalls. In the fall, bald eagles and golden eagles arrive to feed on salmon. Visitors can also enjoy hiking, cross-country skiing, swimming, boating, and fishing.

8   **Mesa Verde National Park** was once the home of Native American cliff dwellers. Carved into the tall canyons, these stone cliff palaces housed the Anasazi [on•uh•sah´•zee]. These Native Americans lived in the area from A.D. 550 to about 1300. Some of the dwellings have more than 50 rooms and are two or three stories high. Mesa Verde National Park is located in Colorado. But it is close to Colorado's borders with New Mexico, Utah, and Arizona. In Spanish, *mesa* means "table" and *verde* means "green." Spanish explorers probably named this park for the flat look of its forest. Park visitors can camp and tour the cliff dwellings by car or tour bus.

9   **Sequoia National Park** is home to some of the world's oldest living trees. Some of the giant sequoias are more than 3000 years old. Looking straight up from the foot of one of them is like looking up at a 25-story building. The park's most famous tree is the General Sherman, named for Civil War hero William T. Sherman. At 272 feet high, it measures 101 feet around the trunk. Another feature of this park is Mount Whitney. It's the highest mountain in the United States outside of Alaska. Visitors can go hiking and mountain climbing. They can also enjoy horseback riding, snowshoeing, and downhill and cross-country skiing.

10   **Yellowstone National Park** lies in Wyoming and borders Montana and Idaho. It's the oldest and one of the most popular of our national parks. Yellowstone is

known mainly for its many geysers [gy´•zerz] and hot springs. The most famous geyser is Old Faithful. It shoots streams of hot water into the air about every 70–80 minutes. These jets of water can reach a height of 150 feet! Yellowstone has beautiful lakes, rivers, and waterfalls, too. People also come to see bears, deer, bighorn sheep, antelope, and buffalo. Bears have been known to come right up to cars and beg for food. But park rangers ask that visitors just watch the bears from afar. Besides sightseeing, visitors can enjoy boating and fishing, nature programs, hiking, and bird-watching.

11   **Yosemite National Park** lies on the western slope of California's Sierra Nevadas. Yosemite Valley is known for its deep, straight-walled canyon. Cliffs rise up to surround the canyon. One such cliff has been named El Capitan. Waterfalls plunge hundreds of feet. The water flows to a flat river valley that was carved by ancient glaciers. The area offers sweeping views of the mountains, meadows, and lakes. Visitors can hike into the backcountry and to the tops of many waterfalls. One trail leads to Glacier Point, which rises to 7200 feet!

12   **Great Smoky Mountains National Park** is about one hour's drive from Knoxville, Tennessee, and from Asheville, North Carolina. It is within one day's drive of almost all the large cities of the East and Midwest. Except for a road that goes through them, the Smoky Mountains stand unbroken for about 70 miles. They are among Earth's oldest mountains and rise to more than 6000 feet. Hikers can follow about 900 miles of trails winding along clear streams and waterfalls. Plant life is lush and varied, with more kinds of trees than in all of Europe. The mountain valleys seem to be screened by a bluish or smokelike mist. This look has given the Smokies their name.

Visiting the Parks

13   The national parks are owned by the people—this means you. A trip to any of the parks is a great way to

see the country. Most of the parks are open year-round, except in bad weather. Many charge a small entrance fee but offer discount rates to seniors.

14   You can drive to the parks or reach them by bus or train. There are usually hotels or motels nearby, and many of the parks have campgrounds. You can write to the National Park Service in Washington, D.C., for information on all the parks.

15   We're lucky that people who cared about the land worked to get laws passed that saved these areas for the public to enjoy. It's up to us to continue caring. We can do our part as visitors to the parks by not littering in them. We can also vote for programs that keep these natural wonders beautiful for future generations.

Questions

1. When did the National Park Service begin?
2. What is special about the Carlsbad Caverns?
3. What river runs through the Grand Canyon?
4. Who used to live in Mesa Verde?
5. What is "Old Faithful"?

Synonym/Antonym Search

1. Find sentences that have synonyms for the following words: *consider, created, unbelievable, investigate, houses.*

2. Rewrite the section that describes Yosemite National Park, substituting synonyms for as many words as you can. Compare your paragraph with a friend's. Did you choose synonyms for the same words? Did you choose the same or different synonyms?

3. Find the sentences in the selection with the following words: *earliest, unique, thrilling, deep.* Rewrite each sentence, using an antonym for the italicized word. You will need to reword the sentences.

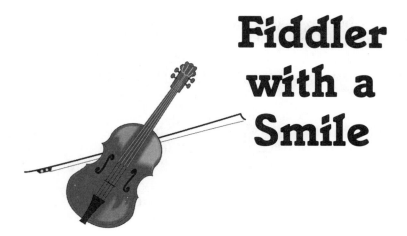

Fiddler with a Smile

How did a boy who was seriously disabled become a world-famous violinist?

1 Itzhak [eet´•tsahk] Perlman is a world-famous violinist from Israel. He also is known as a spokesperson for the disabled.

2   If you asked fellow musicians about Itzhak Perlman, they would likely first mention his cheerful personality. Then they might rave about his musical skills. Last, they might tell you that he is disabled. He cannot walk without the aid of braces and crutches.

Illness Strikes

3 Perlman's paralysis [puh•ral´•ih•sis] is the result of polio. In 1949, when he was four years old, a polio epidemic hit parts of Israel. Polio vaccines [vak•seens´] were not yet in use. At that time, the treatment for polio called for exercising the patient's limbs in warm water. In time, the boy regained strength in his hands and arms. But his legs never fully recovered.

4   Perlman was a determined child. For endless hours, he practiced walking with heavy braces. After some

months, he was able to return to school and rejoin his many friends on the playground. Although he couldn't run as before, Perlman did not feel sorry for himself. And he had something special to keep him busy—music.

A Natural Gift

5   The Perlman family loved music. The sounds of operas and symphonies filled their small apartment in Tel Aviv. So it was natural for Perlman's parents to give their son music lessons. The boy began to study the violin. It would not only keep him occupied but also serve as physical therapy.

6   At the music academy, Perlman's teachers soon realized the boy had unusual ability. He was only 10 when he gave his first solo performance with a well-known orchestra. Musicians from other countries often came to Israel to perform. When they learned of the new violin prodigy [prah´•dih•jee], many people went to hear Perlman play.

7   At about the same time, a popular television show in the United States was looking for talent. The show's host was Ed Sullivan. Each week's program included a variety of acts. Dancers, comedians, singers, and many other musicians performed. Rudolf Nureyev [noo•ray´•yuf], Elvis Presley, and Maria Callas were among them.

A Visit to the United States

8   Sullivan had an idea for a show with young performers. On a talent search, he went to a concert in Haifa [high´•fah], Israel. He watched a smiling, stocky boy with crutches come onstage. Sullivan was impressed by the boy's performance. He invited Perlman to perform on American television.

9   Ed Sullivan then asked Perlman to join his three-month tour of gifted young musicians. It was called The Ed Sullivan Caravan of Stars. When the tour ended,

Perlman and his mother moved to New York City. They decided that New York was now the best place for Perlman to continue his music education. Perlman's father later joined them in the United States.

10   With help from sponsors, Perlman was able to enter Juilliard [joo´•lee•ard], a world-famous music school. One teacher who auditioned him said, "The development of skill was so far beyond that of any other child, it was just startling. He had large hands, a fluent bowing arm, as well as superb timing and exceptional coordination [koh•or•din•ay´•shun]."

Rising Star

11   Perlman was on his way to a career as a concert violinist. When he was 17, his teachers felt he was ready to play at Carnegie Hall. He made his debut [day•byoo´] on March 5, 1963. The young artist looked forward to the critics' reviews. But because of a newspaper strike, the concert went unreported. News of the violin prodigy got around by word of mouth anyway.

12   In 1964, Perlman entered an important competition. It offered prize money and the chance to appear with major symphony orchestras. Out of 40 applicants, the judges chose 10 semifinalists. Perlman was the youngest. He won first place playing the music of Mozart [moh´•tsart], Tchaikovsky [chy•kawv´•skee], Bach [bock], and other famous composers.

13   For the contest, Perlman had borrowed a very rare 200-year-old violin. As people came up to congratulate him afterward, he set the violin aside. When he went to pick it up later, the violin was gone. The next day, it was found in a local pawn shop and quickly returned to Perlman. For only $15, someone had pawned the priceless instrument!

14   Newspapers reported the theft along with rave reviews of Perlman's performance. One critic said: "He

is the major talent among the younger generation of fiddlers and the missing link in the great tradition."

15   Perlman's career took off like a meteor. His schedule was soon filled with many live performances, recordings, television shows, and practice. His guest appearances on television have included *60 Minutes, The Frugal Gourmet* [goor•may´], and *Sesame Street.* Imagine how much fun he had playing the violin for Oscar the Grouch!

Like Everyone Else

16   With all his fame, Perlman never forgot about the special problems that people with disabilities face every day. He serves on committees and speaks to groups. He tells them that disabled people want to be treated like everyone else. He speaks out about the lack of handicapped facilities in hotels and public buildings. Perlman's efforts have made building designers more aware of the needs of the disabled.

17   Perlman likes to visit schools and hospitals. He cheers up the children with jokes. His sense of humor carries over to concert audiences, too. Once, during a performance, a string on his violin broke. Instead of going backstage, Perlman stayed on to chat with the audience while he repaired the violin string.

18   Itzhak Perlman ranks high among the outstanding violinists of the 20th century. His playing, as well as his personality, is filled with vigor and joy. His disability could have turned Perlman into an unhappy person. Instead, he faces the world with a smile.

Questions

1. How old was Itzhak Perlman when he first soloed with a major symphony orchestra?
2. How has Perlman helped the causes of disabled people?
3. How did Perlman come to first perform on national U.S. television?
4. Why was there no newspaper review of Perlman's Carnegie Hall debut?

Using Context Clues

1. What did Itzhak Perlman do to show that he was a "determined" child?
2. What is a prodigy?
3. In what ways did Perlman's career "take off like a meteor"?

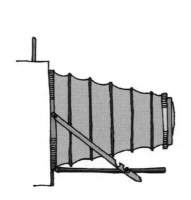

The Woman Behind the Lens

How did Dorothea Lange change history with a picture?

1   The year was 1913. Dorothea Lange had never taken a photograph. She had never even held a camera. She had just finished high school. But Lange already knew what she wanted out of life. She wanted to be a photographer.

Starting from Scratch

2   Lange got to work on her dream. She needed to learn everything about her chosen field. So she went to work for a series of photographers. She learned something from each of them. Lange studied under Clarence White, who taught her an important lesson. Each photograph, he said, should speak for itself.

3   In 1918, Lange made plans for a trip around the world. She hoped to take photos to help pay her way. But in San Francisco, all her money was stolen. She had to give up the trip. Instead, she found a job. She saved her money and made many friends. In 1920, with the help of a friend, Lange opened her own portrait studio.

4　　For the next 10 years, most of the pictures Lange took were of rich people. Her skills were good, and her business was a success. But to her, something was missing. She wasn't always pleased with her work.

5　　Then, in 1929, the Great Depression began. Millions of people lost their jobs. Many lost their homes and farms. Whole families had little or nothing to eat. Lange saw the suffering all around her. It was hard for her to see this misery and still work among the rich. She gave up her portrait business. She took her camera out of the studio and into the real world. Lange said she would now photograph "all kinds of people."

Photographing the Poor

6　On her first day on the streets, Lange took a famous photo. She called it "White Angel Bread Line." It shows a man waiting in line for free soup. There was no soup left. Lange captured the man's look as he was turned away. He is leaning on a railing holding a cup. He looks careworn and very grim. The photo shows how many people felt during the Great Depression.

7　　Lange caught other images of pain and suffering. She went where poor people worked and lived. She took many photos of the awful working conditions in factories. But her specialty was showing the hard life of farm workers.

8　　The goal wasn't just to show that these people were poor. Lange also wanted to get inside these workers. She later said she wanted to catch "their pride, their strength, their spirit" on film.

9　　One day in 1936, she passed a pea-pickers' camp. She stopped to look around. Then Lange took her most famous photograph. Called "Migrant Mother," it shows a woman staring off into space. She is holding a baby on her lap. Two older children bury their faces in her shoulder. The photo shows the mother's deep worry. It also shows her courage.

World War II

10   During World War II, Lange continued to show how some people suffered. Japanese Americans, or Nisei [nee•say´], were born in the United States. But their parents had come from Japan. During the war, the United States and Japan were enemies.

11   Many Americans didn't trust the Nisei. Neither did President Franklin D. Roosevelt. The Nisei had broken no laws. Yet they were locked in prison camps. Roosevelt's order was a black page in American history. Dorothea Lange recorded the results on film.

Her Art Lives On

12   Lange called herself a photographer. Only toward the end of her life did she think of herself as an artist. But Lange *was* an artist long before that time. Through her camera, she was able to show the power of the human spirit.

13   In 1965 the Museum of Modern Art in New York honored Dorothea Lange. The show featuring her works was a first. No other woman photographer had ever held that honor. It is sad that Dorothea Lange died three months before the show opened.

14   The force of her work lives on. Lange's photos of the Nisei were part of a 1972 art show. People who saw these telling photos felt ashamed. One critic wrote that the photos "convey the feelings of the victims as well as the facts of the crime."

Questions

1. What was unusual about Lange's decision to become a photographer?
2. Why did Lange give up her studio work?
3. What kind of people did Lange photograph during the Great Depression?
4. What was unusual about the 1965 honor Lange received from the Museum of Modern Art in New York?

Spelling Word Alert

1. Find the sentences that have the plurals of these words: *photo, factory, child.* Write the singular and plural forms of the words as the headings for three lists: (1) plurals formed by adding *-s;* (2) plurals formed by adding *-es;* and (3) plurals formed by changing the spelling of the singular form. Write words from the selection in the lists.

2. Reread the selection and find as many words as you can that have the *f* sound somewhere in the word. Write each word and underline the letter or letters that spell the sound. Remember, the *f* sound can be spelled *f, ff, ph,* or *gh.* Write a sentence using words that have the *f* sound spelled both *ph* and *gh.*

3. Find words in the selection to which you can add the suffixes *-ful, -ous,* and *-ly.* Write a sentence using each of the new words.

4. Look through the selection to find three possessive nouns, or nouns that show ownership. Answer these questions for each word: Who is the possessor? What is possessed?

Setting the Sky on Fire

What's behind a great show of fireworks?

1 The night explodes in color and light. Streaks of red, white, and gold flash across the sky. A huge boom comes with it. A crowd watches from the ground. Sounds of "oooh" and "aaah" can be heard along with claps and cheers.

2 Almost everyone enjoys watching fireworks. What would Fourth of July celebrations be without them?

History

3 The Chinese sent up fireworks more than 1000 years ago. That tells us the Chinese knew how to use the black powder that goes into making fireworks. Gunpowder is made from black powder, too. But gunpowder wasn't used until the invention of the first muskets and cannons in the 1300s. So we know that people used black powder for fun long before they used it to kill.

4 Word of fireworks spread from China into Europe during the Middle Ages. An English monk, Roger Bacon, wrote about making fireworks in 1242. However,

Bacon thought they were so dangerous that he wrote the instructions in secret code.

Black Magic

5 Making the black powder that goes into fireworks hasn't changed much over time. It is 75 parts saltpeter, 15 parts charcoal, and 10 parts sulfur. All it takes is a spark or fuse to set it off. The mixture burns fast. Gases given off by the fire gush into the air and cause a blast.

6 Setting off black powder makes a bright light. The light itself won't have any color, though. Color is determined by the length of the light rays. To make the different rays, certain metal salts are added to the fireworks. Sodium makes a yellow-orange color. Strontium [stron´•she•uhm] makes red. Copper makes blue and barium, green. When you add magnesium [mag•nee´•zee•uhm] and aluminum powder, it makes the colors glow. Now you know why fireworks are called "chemistry dressed up in flashy clothing."

7 A really rich, blue flame is the hardest to make. A blue flame calls for copper chloride, which won't work if it gets too hot. Getting the blue just right is an art. Purple isn't easy to make either, because the rays for that color are the shortest. So when you see good blue or purple fireworks, you know that the fireworks artists are experts.

Shell Shock

8 Fireworks zoom into the air as shells packed in tubes. Most makers of American and European fireworks use a ball-shaped shell. Lighting the black powder at the bottom of the shell sends it into the air. At the same time, a fuse lights. Once in the air, the fuse goes off and breaks open the shell. The hot gases push out the "stars," sending a shower of light and color into the sky. The "boom" sound comes a few seconds later because sound doesn't travel as fast as light.

9   One kind of shell, called a *salute,* makes only a flash of light and a loud boom. Other shells contain more than one part. As each part goes off, it lights the next part, which creates one burst after another in the sky.

All Shapes and Sizes

10   Have you ever seen fireworks in a pinwheel shape? That shape starts as a long paper tube rolled up tight. Once in the air, the stars pop from the shell and spin in fancy shapes. The way the shell is packed into the tube determines the shape of fireworks. The Japanese kind of shell also sends up a shell in a tube. In this case, the black powder lies in the center of the ball, not at the bottom. This sets off the stars in a round, even shape. It may even set off a trail of light. And if there is more than one color chemical in the shell, the trail will change colors as it goes off.

Family Secrets

11   The secrets of making fireworks have been well kept over the years. Families have passed down information to their children, their children's children, and so on. Even today, most of the world's great fireworks are made by just a few family businesses.

12   The famous fireworks families in the United States are the Gruccis of New York, the Zambellis of Pennsylvania, the Rozzis of Ohio, and the Souzas of California. Only in recent years have fireworks been studied much outside of these families. These studies have helped make fireworks more dazzling, more colorful, and even safer.

Being Careful

13   Safety remains a problem, though, in the care and handling of fireworks. Even small ones can be quite dangerous if they're used carelessly. After every Fourth of July, there are new tragic stories about fireworks

usage gone wrong. That is why the laws are tough when it comes to selling and handling fireworks.

14   Owners of fireworks firms work hard at being careful. One spark in a fireworks plant can blow everything up. In one plant, workers must touch a copper plate as they enter. This removes any electrical charge from a person's body. Inside, workers take care not to rub against each other. And they wouldn't even think of lighting a match!

15   In 1983, one spark set an entire plant on fire, killing two people. Since the accident, the plant owners purchase shells from smaller companies. That way, the most dangerous work is already done.

Enjoy the Show

16   Should just anyone try making fireworks? Of course not. Most of us should not even try to set off the kinds of fireworks available for purchase. Even a simple sparkler gets hot enough to burn a person very badly. The work of setting the sky on fire is best left to trained professionals. We have only to sit back and enjoy the show.

Questions

1. What makes the color in fireworks?
2. Why does the sound of the blast come after the light?
3. What determines the shape of fireworks?
4. Why are there tough laws about selling and using fireworks?

Recalling Details

1. How many years ago did the Chinese use fireworks?
2. What is the "recipe" for making the black powder that goes into fireworks?
3. Which colors are the hardest to make?

The Birth of the Modern Olympics

Why were the Olympic Games revived?

1   The first official Olympic Games took place in Olympia, Greece, in 776 B.C. Some games were held to honor the gods. Others were offerings of thanksgiving. The games were held for hundreds of years. They went on even after the Romans took over Greece in A.D. 146. When the games first began, the athletes were amateurs [am´•uh•turz]. But as time passed, the games grew more professional. Athletes began to compete for personal glory. Many winners put up statues to honor themselves. The original purpose of the games had become lost.

2   As a result, the public grew disgusted and lost interest in the games. In A.D. 394, the games finally came to an end. A Roman emperor outlawed them. The Olympics, said the ruler, had become corrupt.

Pierre de Coubertin

3   For 1500 years the games remained dead. But thanks to one man from France, they came back to life. The man's name was Baron Pierre de Coubertin

[pyair duh•koo•bair•tan´]. He wanted very much to revive the ancient Olympics. However, he thought the Olympics should be more than just fun and games. They should fulfill a higher purpose.

4   De Coubertin wanted the games to promote peace among nations. "Sport is not a luxury," he said. "It is a necessity. Let us bring the nations together for friendly [games]. . . ."

5   De Coubertin felt that the games should serve to teach the young. Like the Greeks of old, he knew the importance of balancing the growth of both mind *and* body. De Coubertin also hoped that the Olympics would inspire the young. The goal of the games, he said, was "to create a way of life based on the joy of effort."

6   De Coubertin believed in fair play and in the "spirit of competition." He once said, "The most important thing is not to win, but to take part." He compared this idea to life. "[It is] not the triumph, but the struggle. The essential thing is not to have conquered, but to have fought well."

Selling His Ideas

7 Selling his idea for the modern Olympics wasn't easy. In 1892, de Coubertin began his tireless campaign [kam•pane´] to revive the games. At first, no one cared much. But de Coubertin would not give up.

8   Two years later, in 1894, de Coubertin brought together 79 delegates from 12 countries. They met to discuss a revival of the Olympic Games. After a passionate plea by de Coubertin, nine nations gave him their full support. The first modern games were set for 1896. The nations agreed that the games would be held every four years in great cities of the world.

9   De Coubertin wanted the first Olympics to be held in France. Others, however, felt that Greece was a better choice, since the Greeks had started the games.

De Coubertin agreed, and in return, France hosted the second Olympics.

The IOC

10 When they had first met in 1894, the nine nations who voted to revive the games also set up the International Olympic Committee, or IOC. The IOC's purpose is to look after the growth and improvement of the Olympics. The members of the IOC were free from outside pressure. No nation could tell the committee how to run the Olympics.

11   De Coubertin thought the IOC's first president should be Greek. The man chosen was Demetrius Vikelas [duh•mee´•tree•uhs vee´•kuh•luhs], who began his term in 1894. In 1896, de Coubertin took over the job and held it for 30 years.

The 1896 Olympics

12 The first modern Olympic Games, held in Athens, Greece, were a great success. King George I of Greece opened the games. More than 60,000 fans packed the stands on opening day.

13   Thirteen countries competed in the games. Only nine sports were involved. They included some of the original Olympic sports such as running and wrestling. But modern sports such as lawn tennis and cycling were also scheduled.

14   Francis Lane, an American, won the first event. He ran 100 meters in 12.5 seconds and won a silver medal for his skill. At that time, only one type of medal was awarded—a silver medal.

Olympic Customs

15 As president of the IOC, de Coubertin made changes to the Olympics that are still in use today. Starting with the 1908 games, the top *three* finishers got medals— gold, silver, and bronze. Both the five-ringed Olympic flag and the Olympic oath were first used in 1920.

16   In later years, the IOC added more customs. The lighting of the Olympic flame began with the 1928 games. So did the custom of releasing a flock of doves as a sign of hope for world peace.

17   The first Winter Olympics were held in 1924. Since then, new winter and summer sports have been added to the games. The number of athletes who compete has increased over time. In 1896, 311 men took part. Now thousands of athletes, both male and female, enter the games. Women first took part in the Olympics in 1900, playing lawn tennis. Today the Olympics involve almost all nations of the world. The games have grown in ways de Coubertin never dreamed of.

The Fate of de Coubertin's Ideals

18   The old games died out when they grew too professional. De Coubertin did not want to see them end once again. So for a long time, the modern games were open only to amateurs. Athletes took part for the love of sports. That ideal, however, is gone; the modern Olympics are now open to anyone. The U.S.A. basketball Dream Team (in 1992, 1996, and 2000), made up of professional athletes, was not what de Coubertin had in mind.

19   Other ideals have also fallen by the wayside. It no longer seems enough just to compete. Everyone wants to *win*. Fans love the winners and forget the losers. Sadly, the drive to win has corrupted the ideal of fair play. Some athletes have used drugs to increase their chances of winning. In spite of these lost ideals, however, the Olympic games remain as popular as ever.

20   De Coubertin died in 1937. His body is buried in Lausanne [lo•zan´], Switzerland, but his heart rests at Olympia, Greece.

Questions

1. Why did the first Olympic Games end?
2. Why did Pierre de Coubertin want to revive the games?
3. What ideals did Pierre de Coubertin want to promote?
4. What is the IOC? What purpose does it serve?
5. What has happened to the ideals of Pierre de Coubertin?

Identifying Sequence

1. How long after de Coubertin began his efforts to revive the games were the first modern Olympics held?
2. When were the Olympic flag and oath added to the games—before or after the first lighting of the Olympic flame?
3. Number these events in the order in which they happened.

   _____ Pierre de Coubertin dies.

   _____ The ancient Olympics come to an end.

   _____ The first Winter Olympics are held.

   _____ The International Olympic Committee is formed.

   _____ Romans take over Greece.

   _____ The U.S.A. basketball Dream Team competes.

   _____ Women begin to take part in the Olympics.

Habitat for Humanity

How does Habitat for Humanity help people in need?

1 A decent home. A safe neighborhood. An affordable mortgage. These have always been part of the American Dream. Yet for many families, this dream seems impossible. These are families in need who struggle to pay their bills and to save money. They cannot afford to buy a house.

2 Such families might lose hope. They may feel that the American Dream is out of reach or that it has passed them by.

A Helping Hand

3 For more than 20 years, a group has helped needy families reach this dream. The group is called Habitat for Humanity. Millard and Linda Fuller, a couple from Georgia, founded the group in 1976. Habitat for Humanity is a nonprofit group. It has one goal: to get rid of poverty-level housing and homelessness around the world.

4   The goal is great. But Habitat for Humanity moves toward it step by step. Since 1976, the group has built or fixed up more than 50,000 homes. These homes shelter about 250,000 people around the world.

How It Works

5   As a nonprofit group, Habitat for Humanity relies on gifts and volunteers. It seeks donations of money, land, and supplies. To keep building costs low, the group tries to get as many gifts as possible. In turn, the group can sell the homes at a very low price. Habitat for Humanity passes the savings on to home buyers. The average price for a three-bedroom home is $38,000.

6   It takes hard work to get donations. Habitat for Humanity tries to raise money through fundraisers. Habitat workers ask cities and wealthy landowners to donate land.

7   The group also seeks gifts from building supply companies. It asks for any materials a company can spare. For example, one company might donate windows, carpeting, or paint. Another company might provide nails or tools.

8   Finally, the group must find volunteer builders. It needs skilled workers. But it uses unskilled workers too. Habitat trains workers on the job, so it welcomes anyone who will pick up a hammer.

The Homeowner's Role

9   Habitat for Humanity works hard to find just the right homeowners. The staff screens each person who wants to buy a home. A family must meet several conditions to be a homeowner. The family must be needy, but it must have some income. Homeowners get an interest-free loan from the Habitat group. They must be able to make monthly payments to pay back the loan in 20 years. These payments are used to fund other Habitat homes.

10   Homeowners also must be willing to work as partners with Habitat for Humanity. They put in their share of "sweat equity." In other words, they must pitch in and help the Habitat workers. Homeowners must help get donations, run the group office, or build homes. Each owner must put in about 500 hours of sweat equity.

11   Albertha Whiteside bought a Habitat home in 1993. As part of her sweat equity, she answered Habitat's phones and sent out newsletters. She also helped frame and hang drywall in her new house. "This is where I learned to pound my first nail," she says with pride.

12   Habitat for Humanity is not a giveaway program. It is a partnership. Habitat becomes a partner with the homeowner. The result is decent housing that is safe and affordable.

Happy Endings

13   The partnership has other results. One example is the chance for buyers to learn useful home management skills. The Habitat program offers workshops for buyers. In them, buyers learn to maintain their homes and to budget their money.

14   Perhaps the best result is the program's effect on families. Buyers say that home ownership greatly improves their lives. Whiteside says that living in the new home has changed her family. Her children are happier, and her marriage has improved. She feels better about herself too. "I've always been a positive person," she said. "But I'm much happier and more relaxed now."

15   Whiteside also notes a big difference between renting and owning. Owning has taught her to budget and save. For minor repairs, Whiteside now depends on herself instead of a landlord. "I'm more mature, more responsible, and more independent," she says.

16   Rena Bligen agrees. "Habitat was the answer to our prayers," she says. Countless others are quick to praise the Habitat program.

A Worldwide Program

17 Habitat for Humanity began as a small group but grew quickly. It now has 1300 branches in the United States, with branches in all 50 states. The program's 250 more branches around the world build houses in more than 50 nations.

18   The program got an unexpected boost in the 1980s. President Jimmy Carter ran for reelection in 1980, but he lost. After this defeat, he and Mrs. Carter joined Habitat for Humanity. His work helped promote the program. Because of the Carters, the program became better known, and many people joined it.

19   The Fullers founded Habitat as a Christian ministry. It still has a Christian focus. In some ways, however, it cuts across the boundaries of religion. "Over the last 20 years, it has really spread out across church lines," says one Habitat director. "There are many people [involved with Habitat] who have no affiliation to a particular church. These are people who still want to find ways to help their fellow human beings."

Questions

1. How long has Habitat for Humanity been in existence?

2. How does Habitat for Humanity keep the cost of its houses down?

3. What does Habitat for Humanity require of home buyers?

4. What famous Americans are involved with Habitat for Humanity?

Recognizing Stated Concepts

1. What is the goal of Habitat for Humanity?

2. How is Habitat for Humanity part of a partnership?

3. List two ways in which Habitat for Humanity changes homeowners' lives.

The World's Longest Railway

What region of the world takes more than a week to cross by train?

1 In 1863, the United States began work on a transcontinental railroad. Rails already ran from the East Coast to Omaha, Nebraska. The new track would extend from Omaha to California. In 1869, six years later, the monumental task was completed. The workers had to cope with huge mountains, deep canyons, and miles of desert. The track ran halfway across the country.

2 As great as that project was, the Russians tried something even greater. They wanted to build a railroad across Siberia [sigh•beer´•ee•uh]. The entire United States could fit inside Siberia, with 1.4 million square miles left over. Imagine the task of building a railroad across that distance!

A Grand Plan

3 The railroad was the grand dream of Czar [zar] Alexander III, the emperor of Russia. He needed the railroad to tie his vast land together. So, in 1891, as

Alexander III laid the first stone, work began. The project called for two work crews. One crew headed east and the other crew, west. Starting from opposite coasts and working inward, the two work crews planned to meet at a point in the middle.

4   Plans called for the track to run from Chelyabinsk [chi•lyah´•binsk] in the west to Vladivostok [vlad•uh•vos´•tok] in the east, near the Pacific coast. That distance would make the railroad the longest in the world—by far! It would cover 4607 miles. The United States railroad was less than a third of that length.

5   Immigrant Irish and Chinese workers built the United States railroad. But the Russians used mostly convicts and exiles to build theirs. The poor job these men did would cause trouble with derailments in the future.

Working Conditions

6 As it was, the railroad workers faced many problems. They had to cross wide rivers and climb steep grades. In some places, the workers had to dig through permafrost. Permafrost, found just below the surface in frigid lands, is a layer of dirt that is frozen year-round.

7   Siberia is well known for its cold winters. This region has some of the lowest temperatures in the world. Forty degrees below zero Fahrenheit is common. At times, the air dips to 60 degrees below zero. Siberia's summers are not easy either. They can be brutally hot, with temperatures often soaring above 100 degrees. Even springtime, bringing ankle-deep mud, can be a problem.

8   Many workers died building this railroad. The work itself killed some of them. The harsh weather killed others. As if that weren't bad enough, a few other workers fell prey to Siberian tigers.

Political Problems

9   Nature was not the only hurdle in building the railroad. Politics caused trouble too. At first, the Russians wanted a route that passed through Russian land only. But in 1896, they signed a treaty with China. One outcome of the treaty shortened the route of the railroad. Part of the track would cut through the north of China.

10   Then, in 1904, war broke out between Russia and Japan. The fighting ended a year later when the Japanese crushed the Russians. Japan also took over the northern part of China. The Russians lost control of that land and the tracks that ran through it. So the Russian railroad would not cut through China, after all. The Russians returned to the old plan for an all-Russian route. At last, in 1917, the railroad was finished. It had taken more than 25 years to build.

Riding the Rails

11   The railroad opened before it was finished. By the end of 1900, trains began to make trips. But there were problems all along the way. Steep grades near the southern shore of Lake Baikal [by•kall´] made it hard to lay tracks in that region. So passengers had to get off the train and cross the lake by ferryboat. In the end, the Russians had to build 38 tunnels through the mountains.

12   The biggest problems, however, were derailments. The trains couldn't be trusted to stay on the tracks. On an average trip, a train would jump the tracks twice. Operators at the time had the good sense to run the trains slowly. The average top speed was just 15 miles per hour. At that slow speed, a derailment didn't often hurt people. But the snail-like pace annoyed travelers. If all went well, a trip across the continent was supposed to take two weeks. Instead, the trip always took longer than three weeks to complete.

The Trans-Siberian Railroad Today

13   Through the years, the Russians improved the Trans-Siberian Railroad. A second set of tracks was laid by 1939 and is still in use today.

14   Now people can hop on a train in Moscow and ride it all the way east to the Sea of Japan. The railroad is, of course, much more reliable today than in the past. But even a smooth trip takes at least 170 hours—more than seven days—to complete.

15   For true railroad buffs, riding the Trans-Siberian Railroad is a must. Most of these people take the trip just to say that they did it. Surely, no one takes the trip for the scenery. At least, no one takes it for the *variety* of scenery: Siberia is one vast, empty plain. Whoever made up the phrase "the middle of nowhere" must have had Siberia in mind. As one writer put it, there is "nothing but hut, tree, hut, filing by with the dull rhythm of a forced march."

16   Still, the railroad has played a vital role in the development of Russia. It has opened up Siberia to settlers. It has also helped industry, for Siberia is rich in natural resources. It has large amounts of oil, coal, natural gas, and iron. The railroad route has linked Siberia's mining centers with Russia's main business areas. Without the railroad, Siberia's natural riches would lie untouched and of little use.

17   The railroad has become a lifeline between Siberia and European Russia. This important outcome may have reached beyond even Czar Alexander's greatest dream.

Questions

1. Why did Czar Alexander want a Trans-Siberian railroad?

2. Name two ways in which building the Trans-Siberian Railroad was different from building the U.S. transcontinental railroad.

3. What dangers did the Russian railroad builders face?

4. Why is the trip across Siberia boring?

5. Why is the Trans-Siberian Railroad important to Russia today?

Using Maps and Graphs

1. Find a world atlas that contains a topographical map of Siberian Russia. (A topographical map shows the surface features of a place, such as mountains, rivers, and lakes.) Use the map's key to help you interpret the symbols on the map, then write a paragraph describing Siberia's topography.

2. During the late 1800s, several rail systems were built throughout the world. The Trans-Siberian Railway traveled from Chelyabinsk, Russia, to Vladivostok, Russia; the *Orient Express* ran from Paris, France, to Istanbul, Turkey; and the *Venice Simplon Orient Express* ran from Paris, France, to Venice, Italy. Locate each pair of cities on a map, trace their routes, and use the map's scale to find the number of miles each railway covered.

3. Use the distances you measured above to make a bar graph. Draw a bar to represent the total distance covered by each of the three rail systems. Compare the data. Reread the section "A Grand Plan." Which of the rail systems had more miles of track than the United States' transcontinental railroad?

Hong Kong: An Uncertain Future

Why does Hong Kong—with its impressive past—face an uncertain future?

1 Hong Kong is a tiny island off the southern coast of China. This island has had an interesting past. For centuries it was almost empty. Yet today, nearly six million people live in the Hong Kong area. These people face an uncertain future.

A British Colony

2 Hong Kong began as a small fishing community. Pirates and drug smugglers also used Hong Kong's beautiful harbor. One British leader described Hong Kong as "a barren island with hardly a house upon it."

3 In the 1840s, China and Great Britain were at war. Britain used Hong Kong as a naval base. After Britain won the war, it signed a treaty with China. The treaty gave Britain ownership of Hong Kong.

4 For the next century, the British used the island both as a naval base and as a trading base. Hong Kong thrived. Meanwhile, Britain added Kowloon and Stonecutters Island to its colony in 1860. It later added

the New Territories in 1898. Together, these areas were known as Hong Kong colony.

5   The British did not own the New Territories. Instead, they signed a 99-year lease for the area. After 99 years, Britain would have to give this region back to China.

The Colony Thrives

6 Hong Kong did well under British rule. The people were hardworking and creative in business. The economy boomed, and the future looked bright.

7   In the 1930s, Japan went to war with China. The Japanese invaded China. Hundreds of thousands of Chinese fled to Hong Kong for safety.

8   In 1939, World War II broke out. During the war, the Japanese attacked Kowloon and the New Territories. The British surrendered Hong Kong to the Japanese. However, the Japanese lost the war in the end, and the British regained control of Hong Kong in 1945. By this time, about 600,000 people lived there.

9   After World War II, civil war broke out in China. In 1949, the Communist side won this war. Again, hundreds of thousands of Chinese fled to Hong Kong. They did not want to live under communism. The population of Hong Kong swelled to about 2 million.

10   Immigrants continued to pour into the colony. By 1971, Hong Kong had 4 million people. By 1995, more than 5.5 million lived there. The sleepy fishing village had become a crowded, busy region.

Boomtown

11 Through the years, the immigrants turned Hong Kong into a boomtown. They worked hard for low wages. Investors sank money into Hong Kong. Its manufacturing industry grew. Its banking business grew. It developed a stable free-market economy.

12   Hong Kong became a major center for world trade. The tiny colony carried on more trade than all of China. In fact, it became the eighth-largest trade center in the world.

13   Hong Kong's success made it attractive to the Chinese communists, who wanted the colony to be part of China again. They could have just taken it. The British would not have defended Hong Kong against a military attack. No one, however, wanted a war, least of all the Chinese. They wanted control of a healthy Hong Kong. Why damage the thing they wanted to possess?

An Agreement

14   In September 1984, Britain and China reached an agreement. Britain agreed to return Hong Kong to China. They named a date: July 1, 1997. This was the date when Britain's 99-year lease on the New Territories would end. But now it would be the date when Britain would hand over the rest of the colony as well.

15   The agreement caused a problem. China was communist, but Hong Kong had a free-market economy. How could Hong Kong survive under communist rule? The 1984 agreement tried to fix this problem. The fix would last only for a set time. For at least 50 years, Hong Kong would keep its way of life. It would keep its legal, social, and economic systems. The Chinese invented a slogan for this fix. They called it "one country—two systems."

An Uncertain Future

16   On July 1, 1997, Britain kept its part of the 1984 agreement; it gave Hong Kong colony back to China. "One country—two systems" may not work. China and Hong Kong have different economic systems. In China, the government runs the economy. People do not have much personal wealth. In Hong Kong, people can work hard and earn money. They live well.

17   China and Hong Kong also have different types of government. As a British colony, Hong Kong was not a true democracy. However, its people had a number of freedoms. They had more freedom than their neighbors in China.

18   In 1995, the people of Hong Kong held an election. They elected Democrats to the legislature—for a good reason. They wanted as much democracy as possible before the 1997 handover. The more Democrats in power, they thought, the harder it would be for China to take away people's freedom.

19   The Chinese frowned on the election. They said that they would close the legislature after the takeover. Then they would name a new legislature. The people of Hong Kong would not get to elect the new members. Instead, China would appoint them.

20   In 1996, eight Democrats from Hong Kong flew to the capital of China. They wanted to talk with China's leaders. They planned to ask them not to close the legislature. But the Chinese leaders did not want to talk. They would not even let the eight spokespersons get off the plane.

21   What does all this mean for the future of Hong Kong? The signs are not hopeful, judging from recent events in China. In 1989, the Chinese crushed a freedom movement in their own country. They did it with brutal force. In early 1997, the top Chinese leader died. Changes in leadership make the future even harder to predict. For the present, Hong Kong continues to thrive. But now that Hong Kong again belongs to China, its people wait and wonder what the future holds for them.

Questions

1. How did Great Britain come to control Hong Kong colony?

2. How did Britain's control of the New Territories differ from its control of the rest of the colony?

3. What agreement did Britain reach with China in 1984?

4. What is the meaning of the phrase, "one country—two systems"?

Graphs/Dictionary

1. Skim the selection "Hong Kong: An Uncertain Future" and find the facts about Hong Kong's increasing population. Make a line graph to show how Hong Kong's population has changed over the years. Why do you think the population grew as it did?

2. The selection says "The economy boomed, and the future looked bright." Look up the word *boom* in the dictionary. What two parts of speech can *boom* be? Which meaning of *boom* fits the sentence?

3. Choose four words from the selection that are unfamiliar to you. Use a dictionary to find out their meanings. Write a sentence using each word.

Cambodia's Grand Temple

What makes Angkor Wat one of the world's great treasures?

1   Angkor Wat is among the most important structures in the world. It is in the same class as the Great Wall of China and the pyramids of Egypt. Yet until recently, it was unknown to most people. Little by little, the world is starting to see what a treasure Angkor Wat really is.

Building the Temple

2   The people of Cambodia are known as Khmer [kuh•mair´]. In the ninth century, they decided to build a new capital and chose a place in northwestern Cambodia. The Khmer called their city *Angkor*, which means "capital." The city was built around a temple on a hill. At that time in history, the Khmer practiced the Hindu religion. They believed that a temple was the center of the world.

3   Over the years, Khmer kings added many more temples, forming a large group of buildings. These buildings extended 15 miles from east to west and 8 miles from north to south. The most magnificent

building was Angkor Wat. (The word *wat* means "temple.") Angkor Wat was built by King Suryavarman II, who ruled in the early 12th century.

4   Angkor Wat is the largest temple in the world. Built of stone, the stunning structure stands 200 feet high. A moat 2 1/2 miles wide surrounds the temple.

5   Everything about the temple's design was inspired by Hindu beliefs. For example, the temple's five lotus-shaped towers stand for mountains. Hindus believe that mountains are the dwelling places of the gods. The large moat around the temple is a symbol for the oceans of the world. Beyond these "oceans" lies the outside world. The moat removes and protects the temple from the rest of the world—a design meant to honor the gods. To reach the temple requires crossing a 617-foot bridge. The temple walls are covered with fine sculptures, which show scenes from Hindu stories.

Neglect and Decay

6   In 1177, Angkor was attacked. A neighboring group of people sacked the city. The event made King Jayavarman VII, who ruled at that time, believe that the Hindu gods had failed him. So he built a new capital nearby called Angkor Thom [tom] and dedicated it to Buddhism [boo´•diz•uhm]. Angkor Wat then became a Buddhist shrine, and Buddhist art replaced some of its Hindu art.

7   In spite of the king's efforts, the Khmer empire became weak anyway. Armies from Thailand [tie´•land] kept attacking Angkor. At last, in 1431, these enemy armies captured the city of Angkor. The Khmer abandoned the city and moved south for safety. Certain monks continued to use Angkor Wat for a while. Later, the surrounding jungle slowly overgrew the city and its many temples. Left to the forces of nature, Angkor began to decay. Its temples fell to ruins.

8   That was how things stayed for more than 400 years. Then, in 1860, a French explorer "discovered" the

city, and French scholars began to research the temples' history. The findings soon led others to understand that the temples were worth saving. By the early 1900s, a large-scale program to restore the temples had begun.

9   World Wars I and II slowed work on the temples. Later, the war in Vietnam spilled into Cambodia. Bombs and other ground fighting destroyed much of the country. In spite of all the trouble, Angkor Wat suffered only a few bullet holes. The real damage to it had happened through neglect.

Angkor Wat Today

10   Most of Angkor Wat has been saved. It took much work and a great amount of concrete. The many years of neglect had damaged the temple's foundation. A new concrete foundation had to be poured under the buildings. To support the old sandstone blocks, it was necessary to also build new inside walls of concrete.

11   The years of chaos [kay´•os] and war caused another form of damage—theft. It happened often during the late 1970s, when Pol Pot ruled Cambodia. During Pol Pot's reign of terror, Cambodian communists—called the Khmer Rouge [roozh]—killed more than one million Cambodians. Pol Pot's soldiers also tore through Angkor Wat, taking more than 3500 priceless works of art. They sold most of these pieces to private dealers in Bangkok.

12   For all it has been through, Angkor Wat remains a treasure. Rising grandly out of the jungle, the temple is an important link to Cambodia's past. It also shows the beauty and great depth of the Hindu religion.

A New Problem

13   The importance of Angkor Wat, however, has caused a major dilemma in recent years. Should the temple be protected as a holy shrine, or should it be further opened to tourists?

14   It is not an easy choice. Cambodia is a very poor country; its people could use the money that the tourist trade would bring in. In 1986, Angkor Wat drew only 565 tourists. Ten years later, in 1996, more than 70,000 visitors flocked to see the temple. Such interest meant a large increase in tourist dollars. Now developers want to pave the way for even more tourists in the years to come. They have planned to build luxury hotels along the road leading to Angkor. These builders also put pressure on Cambodian officials to relax laws that limit the areas for building.

15   Not all Cambodians like the changes that are taking place. Tourists have started to leave their mark on Angkor Wat already. Trash litters the grounds. Even worse, some tourists have written graffiti on the temple walls.

16   Many Cambodians are speaking out against the tourist trade. They don't want outsiders pouring into Angkor Wat. "We want visitors to regard [a visit to Angkor Wat] as a pilgrimage," says one Cambodian. "We don't want 20,000 tourists a day." As that person points out, Angkor Wat was not built as a museum but as a sacred place for the people of Cambodia.

Questions

1. What beliefs inspired the building of Angkor Wat?

2. Name two important features of Angkor Wat.

3. Why did the Khmer leave Angkor Wat?

4. What damage has Angkor Wat suffered?

5. What decision must Cambodians make about the future of Angkor Wat?

Dictionary/Index/Using Reference Sources

1. Use a dictionary to compare the meanings and word histories of the words *temple* and *shrine*.

2. Use a thesaurus to find synonyms for the noun *neglect*. In this selection, which synonyms could be substituted for the word *neglect*?

3. Look up the subject *Angkor Wat* in the index of an encyclopedia. Are there subentries about the subject? What other articles are cross-referenced?

4. Would you find *Angkor Wat* listed in the "Geographical Names" section of a dictionary? Why or why not?

The Cold Facts

What is fact and what is myth about fighting the common cold?

1 "They can send an astronaut to the moon, but they can't cure the common cold." How many times have you heard that? It's true that people have landed on the moon. It's also true that after all these years, people on Earth still catch colds. Why can't we get rid of a common ailment that causes *30 billion* lost days of work or school each year?

Virus-Driven

2 Because a virus causes it, the common cold still has no real cure. There are about 200 different cold viruses. Sooner or later you will probably catch a cold caused by one of these viruses. A vaccine [vak•seen´] against one kind of virus does not stop infection by another. But take heart. There is a *sort of* cure for the common cold: time. A cold simply needs to run its course, which takes about a week. All you can do is get through that week as comfortably as you can.

Telltale Signs

3   The first sign of a cold is usually a sore throat. You can
help a sore throat in three ways: by sucking on a cough
drop, using throat spray, or gargling with warm salt
water. These treatments will ease the pain, but they
won't stop a cold from taking hold. Research shows
that mouthwash won't help fight off a cold at all.

4   Next comes the runny, stuffy nose. This is the body's
way of fighting the virus, but you don't have to put up
with it. Using nose drops or sprays can help stop a
runny nose. Although you may have heard differently,
using these medicines will *not* make a cold last longer
than usual. Just take care not to use them for more than
three days. If you do, you may need more and more
drops or spray to keep your nose clear. These medicines
may also raise your blood pressure. You could try cold
pills instead, although doctors say they don't work as
well.

Aches and Pains

5   Fever and body aches also come with some colds. The
best thing to do is rest and drink plenty of water or
juice. Aspirin may help, but it is not good for children.
No longer just a family cure, chicken soup seems to
work wonders for a cold that also brings aches. Some
doctors say the salt in the soup keeps you from drying
out, which makes you feel better. Others say any hot
drink or soup will do the job.

6   A cough often appears near the end of a cold. For a
dry cough that keeps you awake, take simple cough
syrup. A cough drop with menthol may ease a cough
that tickles your throat. If your cold lasts longer than 10
days, you should call a doctor. Chances are that the
cold has become a sinus or ear problem, and you'll
need something stronger than cold medicines to knock
it out.

The Flu

7 Influenza [in•floo•en´•zuh], or the flu, also affects
your nose and throat, but it's different from the
common cold. The flu strikes fast and is more
dangerous. Often hitting harder than a cold, a bout of
flu will likely send you to bed for a week or so. If you
get the flu, you should call a doctor. Better yet, you
should see a doctor *before* you get sick. There are
vaccines for the flu, which is caused by only a few
different viruses.

Staying Healthy

8 The best way to beat a cold is to not catch one. It is
actually harder to get a cold than you might think.
When you're in good health, your body works hard to
fight a virus. Eating well and getting plenty of rest and
exercise are your best defenses against colds.

9   Keep from catching a cold by not letting the virus
enter your body. Don't get too close to someone with a
cold. Spend as little time as possible in places filled
with people, such as a day-care center, an elevator,
and a doctor's office. Even with care, you will likely
catch a cold from someone you live with. This is
especially true if you live with smokers. Get out of
the way when they sneeze or cough. Wash off door
handles, phones, and anything else that smokers
touch. Use your own towel and cup. Whatever you
do, wash your hands often, and use soap. The most
common way to spread a cold is through the hands.
Don't touch your nose or eyes, or you might pass the
10 cold virus right into your body.

Vitamin C will not stop you from catching a cold. It
can, however, make it less of a problem. Some people
take lots of vitamin C at the first sign of a cold. It may
help.

Myths About Colds

11 You have probably heard that you'll catch a cold if you get a chill. An important study showed that this is not true. The study used three groups of people. One group was given nose drops that contained a cold virus. The people in this group then stood in a cold room for one half-hour wearing wet bathing suits. The second group took the same drops but did nothing else. The third group took no drops but stood in the cold room in wet bathing suits. People in the two groups that took the drops caught colds. The third group did not get sick. The chill didn't matter a bit.

12   What about the saying "Feed a cold, starve a fever"? It's not true, either. Someone with a cold or the flu may not feel like eating. There is no good reason for a person who feels that way to eat if he or she is not hungry.

13   Researchers have not given up trying to cure the common cold. Laboratories worldwide are working on a number of possible cures. Perhaps a certain vitamin can help the body fight off colds. Or, there may be a way to kill a virus after it enters the body. Maybe people who are under little stress *can* avoid catching colds better than others. Now and then you may hear that a cure for colds is just around the corner. When that rumor becomes fact, you can bet that everyone will tune in for the details!

Questions

1. What causes the common cold?
2. Why should cold sufferers stop using nasal sprays or drops after three days?
3. Why is a vaccine helpful in preventing the flu but not a cold?
4. What are three ways to avoid getting a cold?

Using Forms/Understanding Consumer Materials

1. A pharmaceutical company plans to develop a new cold-care product, so it wants to know about people's experiences with colds. Create a form that people can fill out quickly and easily that will give the company information it can use. Think about how to handle questions such as these in a checklist or multiple choice format: How long ago did people have a cold? How long did it last? What symptoms did they have? What did they do for the cold? For example, what medicines did they take? What did they like about these medicines? What did they dislike?

2. Consumer publications often rate products to help consumers make wise purchasing decisions. Choose a home health-care product such as throat sprays, adhesive bandages, sports creams, or nonprescription pain relievers. Use a consumer magazine to research the products' ratings. Then choose another home health-care product, create a similar ratings system, and survey your friends and family. Display the results on a grid.

Business Leader: Remedios Diaz-Oliver

How did Remedios Diaz-Oliver go from prisoner to top business leader?

1 Life was easy at first for Remedios Diaz-Oliver [re•mee´•dyos dee´•ahs oh•lee•vuhr´]. Her father was a rich hotel owner in Cuba. When she was a young girl, Diaz-Oliver went with her father on business trips to the United States and to Spain. So she saw countries and cultures other than her own.

2 Diaz-Oliver's native tongue, of course, was Spanish. But she also learned to speak English, French, and Italian. She went to good schools and finished high school a year early. She earned a doctorate [dok´•tuhr•it] in education from the University of Havana. Her plan was to become a teacher.

Trouble in Cuba

3 In 1959, Fidel Castro [fee•del´ kas´•troh] came to power in Cuba. He promised Cubans a better life but gave them a communist dictatorship.

4 Diaz-Oliver's family backed Castro because the old regime [ray•zheem´] had been corrupt. The family had

hoped for better times under Castro, an old family friend. Instead, Castro began to take away people's rights. In 1960, Castro saw Diaz-Oliver. He remembered her from when she was a child. "How are you?" Castro asked.

5   "Surprised," she answered, "that you didn't keep your promises."

6   Perhaps Castro did not jail Diaz-Oliver then because she was pregnant. But in 1961, Castro had her arrested and jailed for a short time. Diaz-Oliver had protested when Castro had people's mail checked. Castro feared an overthrow of his government. So he had inspectors check letters to Cuba for word of any plans for a revolt. When Diaz-Oliver was freed, she fled to the United States with her husband and daughter.

Starting Over

7   Now a refugee [ref•yoo•jee´], Diaz-Oliver was nearly broke and in need of work. She was a teacher but was not certified to teach in the United States.

8   She found a job with Emmer Glass, a firm that sold containers. Diaz-Oliver earned only $10 a day, but she soon saw a chance to better herself. She knew that Emmer Glass wanted to attract buyers from Cuba and other parts of Latin America. Diaz-Oliver's Spanish language skills would be useful to the company.

9   She began to study the container business. She wanted to know all there was to know. She read every book and catalog she could find. Soon she was an expert in the field.

10   Within a year, Diaz-Oliver got a big promotion. Emmer Glass put her in charge of all foreign sales. She sold huge numbers of containers to Central America. Within 10 years, Emmer Glass ranked first among firms that sold containers to places in Central America. Diaz-Oliver's hard work earned her the "E" Award. The "E" stands for Excellence in Export. Diaz-Oliver received

the award from the president of the United States. She was the first Hispanic business leader—male or female—to win this prize.

Dealing with Prejudice

11   One key to Diaz-Oliver's success was staying cool under pressure. Some people did not want to do business with her because she was female. But she never showed anger. Instead, she responded calmly with good humor and did her job well.

12   One male buyer who got Diaz-Oliver on the phone thought she was a secretary. He asked to talk to the boss. Diaz-Oliver told him that she *was* the boss. "I will never do business with a Cuban." She calmly told him that he didn't have to and had him speak with a co-worker.

13   A year later, the man came crawling back. He needed Diaz-Oliver to help him out of a tight spot. She came through for him, and she did it without hard feelings. Soon the two became friends. The client even invited Diaz-Oliver to attend his son's wedding. (The son was marrying a Cuban woman!) The man also recommended her to other clients. Diaz-Oliver once said, "You can't get anything accomplished with anger. Everyone discriminates."

Her Own Company

14   In 1976, Diaz-Oliver took a big step. She and her husband started their own firm, a supplier of glass and plastic bottles. Diaz-Oliver's knowledge and years in the business helped make it a success. In just one year, the company made close to a million dollars in sales. In 1991, sales reached $90 million.

15   She was asked how she became so successful. Diaz-Oliver said, "I don't think [my success] is about being a woman or a minority as much as it is going into the boardroom with the same knowledge as men."

Questions

1. Why did the future look bright for Diaz-Oliver as a young girl?
2. Why was Diaz-Oliver jailed in 1961?
3. What does the "E" in the "E Award" stand for?
4. What did Diaz-Oliver do in 1976?

Analyzing Character/Identifying Main Idea

1. What character traits did Diaz-Oliver exhibit in her early career at Emmer Glass?
2. How did she handle discrimination? What does this show about her character?
3. What is the main idea of the whole selection?

Faith, Family, and Farming

What can we learn from the Amish people? Can their way of life survive in the modern world?

1   The Amish people of Lancaster County, Pennsylvania, share a 300-year-old tradition. Their society is based on faith, family, and farming. Every part of their life, from clothes to work, is part of their faith. And living in our modern world isn't easy.

Their History

2   The ancestors of the Amish belonged to the Swiss Anabaptist religion. They believed in adult, not infant, baptism. In the 1600s, this belief brought punishment by death in many European countries. To avoid persecution, many Anabaptists moved to farms. They wanted to be self-sufficient [suh•fish´•ent]. They worshipped in private homes, not public churches.

3   Jacob Ammann was a church leader who wanted to make some changes. In 1693, he and his followers split from the Anabaptists. They became known as the *Amish.*

4   In the mid-1700s, to escape persecution, the Amish came to America. Here, some of them changed their beliefs. They broke away to start their own sects. Today, Amish live in 22 states and in Canada. The Lancaster County group is the oldest Amish settlement in the world.

5   The Old Order Amish here are the most traditional. Their clothing has hardly changed since Jacob Ammann's time. They use horses to farm and horse-drawn buggies for travel. They still worship in private homes.

The Farms

6 The average Amish farm is 60 acres. This is small enough to farm with a team of horses or mules. But it requires the whole family to work on it. Milk is a main product. Almost all families have a herd of about 50 cows. Farming teaches the children the values of their parents and the importance of hard work.

7   The average Amish family has seven children. When a son marries, his father gives him his own farm. Late autumn is wedding time in Lancaster. Almost 200 couples marry every year, and each couple would prefer to have their own farm. But a farmer can divide his farm only so many times.

8   Lancaster County has excellent farmland. It's close to big cities, such as Philadelphia and Baltimore. For these reasons, many people want to move to this area. The price of land, in turn, has become very expensive. A farmer may not be able to afford a nearby farm for his son. So the young farmer might have to move far from his family and friends.

The Outside World

9 Travel isn't easy for the Amish. Going to church or visiting family in a horse and buggy takes time. As more people move to Lancaster, traffic problems get

worse. Driving a buggy on crowded roads can be dangerous.

10   To those problems, add the tourists. Every summer, about five million tourists visit Amish country. Traffic becomes a nightmare. Most tourists are there to see the Amish, who have to put up with cars and buses full of people staring at them.

11   Tourism has made life difficult in other ways. The Amish must sometimes listen to unkind comments about their clothes and way of life. They must watch their food, homes, and crafts turned into tourist attractions.

Moving Out

12   Because of these pressures, many Amish families have moved away. Leaving the home settlement is hard. Many have lived their whole lives in one place. Farmhouses might be attached to one another. Grandparents live in one, parents in another, and perhaps a third generation next door. Births, weddings, worship, and funerals all take place at home. Children go to the same school. Nearby relatives help one another.

13   After family, the church district is most important to the Amish. It includes about 25 to 35 families. It's kept small so that Sunday services can be held in one house. People from the same district try to move together. When moving, they look for a quiet place with good land. As one member said, "Good soil makes a strong church."

In the Business World

14   For the Amish who stay, there still aren't enough farms. So many Amish have started their own businesses. Some trades, such as blacksmithing, have always existed in the community. Others, such as the roadside vegetable stands, fit in with farming. Still others are aimed at tourists, such as selling quilts and other crafts.

15   The Amish prefer businesses that keep them in their community. Many of their customers are other Amish people. They may not earn as much as they would at outside jobs, but they're with their own people.

16   The Amish are good carpenters. And because the Amish people value hard work, contractors are eager to hire them. Amish call outsiders "the English." The English contractors pick up the men and drive them to work in cars.

17   Some Amish don't like this contact with the English. It takes men away from their families and communities. And their children don't learn farming. As one saying goes, "The lunch pail is the greatest threat to our way of life."

18   Amish women run businesses, too. That's because the high cost of living demands a second income. Women work as cooks and bakers. And many work together making quilts, which have become very popular.

19   Retired farmers often run a business, such as a general store. The Amish rely on the church when they retire. They don't take Social Security money from the government. So the extra money from a business helps out.

Technology

20 The Amish look at new inventions carefully. One member of the community tries out the invention. The community then decides whether it will be good or bad for them. The decision is based on how the invention will affect their beliefs.

21   In the past, some Amish had electricity. But now it is banned. The Amish think electricity makes people less self-sufficient. They fear it will weaken family life and lead to things like watching television. They also fear that electricity might be used to run machinery that would take jobs away from people.

22   Some Amish farmers used to drive tractors. But tractors are expensive. And many farmers were afraid this would lead to some people owning more land than others. Then they would no longer be equals. They also thought that owning tractors would lead to owning cars. Cars might take people far away from the community.

23   Instead of using these things, the Amish have made their own inventions. They have designed windmills, generators, and other aids to run equipment. They have built farm machinery and equipment to repair the machinery.

What's Ahead?

24   Many things threaten the Amish community. They are being pushed off their land by newcomers and high prices. Jobs away from the farm weaken their traditions. Money threatens their values.

25   One Amish man says, "Families are not as tightly knit as they used to be. No one wants to work seven days a week anymore. But you can't get away from it—they just aren't making any more land, and there's no better place to raise a family than a farm. We must either adapt to Lancaster County's ways or move."

26   Some Amish feel they are being tested. They want to preserve their way of living. If not in Lancaster County, perhaps they will find another place with peace and good farmland.

Questions

1. Where is the oldest Amish community in America?
2. What is the main kind of work the Amish do?
3. What do the Amish use for transportation?
4. Why do builders like to hire Amish workers?
5. Why do some young Amish couples have to move away?

Comparing and Contrasting/Drawing Conclusions

1. How does the daily life of an Amish family compare with the daily life of your family?
2. In what ways is the Amish way of worshipping like other religions? In what ways is it different?
3. Why do the Amish think it is important to be self-sufficient?
4. Do you think the Amish way of life can survive in the modern world? Why or why not?
5. What do you think is most important to the Amish? Explain your answer.

Battle of the Ballot

How would you feel if you had lived at a time when women couldn't vote?

1 Picture yourself living in 1848. Women in the United States aren't allowed to vote. They can't own property. They can't serve on juries or even go to most colleges!

2 Many women were upset about these things. They knew that change had to come, and soon. In 1848, about 300 women met in Seneca Falls, New York, to hold the first Women's Rights Convention.

3 At this meeting, the women talked about their goals. They wanted to buy property in their own names. Like men, they wanted the right to a good education. Most important, they wanted the right to vote. With the vote, they would be the political equals of men.

4 A few women were nervous about asking for the vote. They couldn't believe they would ever get it. But they decided to work for it anyway.

Banding Together

5 For many years, women had banded together to fight social problems. Many groups had spoken out against

slavery. Others fought to ban alcoholic drinks or to improve education. Word spread about the brave women in Seneca Falls. Other groups joined the fight for women suffrage. Many had gained skills from their group work. Now they used these skills to change the minds of the American public.

Two Leaders

6 Two women stand out as the leaders in the struggle for the right to vote. Neither lived to see the laws changed. But their hard work started the movement. These women refused to let the dream of equal rights die.

7 Elizabeth Cady Stanton was the mother of six children. She was an excellent writer and speaker. Her father had been a judge. As a child, Stanton saw how unfair the law was to women, and she vowed to change it.

8 Mrs. Stanton's best friend was Susan B. Anthony. Anthony grew up in a Quaker family. She had been active in the fight against slavery. She had strong feelings about justice.

9 Anthony taught school for several years. One day, she learned that a male teacher was earning $40 a month while Anthony made only $10. The pay was different only because she was a woman. Her sense of justice told her to work for women's rights.

Call to Action

10 Anthony began to organize women to try to change the law. She planned women's meetings and conventions. She gave speeches written by Stanton, who was often busy with her young children. Anthony felt that people needed to hear her words.

11 In 1869, Anthony and Stanton formed the National Woman Suffrage Association (NWSA). The group's goal was an amendment to the Federal Constitution that gave women the right to vote. That year another

group formed called the American Woman Suffrage Association (AWSA). This group did not work toward one main law for women suffrage. Instead, the AWSA strove for a suffrage amendment to each state constitution.

12   Stanton, Anthony, and many other women spoke to groups of people all over the United States. They urged citizens to write to their leaders. They asked lawmakers to change the laws. They asked men as well as women to sign petitions. The important question put to the public was "If women are citizens, why can't they vote?"

Not Always Welcome

13 Workers for women's rights were not always welcome in places where they gathered to speak. During speeches, people threw eggs and vegetables. They made fun of the women suffragists and called them names. Even many women slammed doors in their faces. Men laughed at what the suffragists said. Newspapers poked fun at the way they dressed. Little by little, however, people's minds began to change. But even after years of work, women still didn't have the right to vote.

14   In 1870, a new amendment to the Constitution granted the vote to male ex-slaves. The new law made the suffragists impatient. In 1872, some women decided to vote anyway. They felt that the new amendment was meant as much for women as for the male ex-slaves. Susan B. Anthony was among this group of women. On November 5, 1872, Anthony walked into a polling place in Rochester, New York. She signed up to vote and demanded a ballot from the election staff. She said that the Constitution gave all the citizens the right to vote. Then she cast her ballot in the presidential election held that year.

15   Later, Anthony wrote these words to Stanton: "Well, I have been and gone and done it, positively voted this morning at 7 o'clock. . . . Now if all our suffrage women would work to this end. . . what strides we might make from now on!"

On Trial

16 Because she had broken the law, Anthony was arrested. She had to stand trial for voting. The judge found her guilty and fined her $100. Anthony said she would never pay the unjust fine. Even so, she was released.

17   In 1875, the Supreme Court considered whether women had the right to vote. They said that the Constitution did *not* give women the right to vote. They *were* citizens, but not *all* citizens had the right to vote. The suffragists were disappointed, but they didn't give up. Now they knew they had to change the Constitution.

Two Groups Unite

18 In 1890, the two major women's rights groups (the NWSA and the AWSA) united. They formed the National American Woman Suffrage Association. For the next 29 years, this group worked to change the Constitution.

19   Over and over, the suffragists sent congressmen copies of the "Anthony Amendment." This amendment would give women the right to vote. The suffragists urged people to write to their congressmen. They stood outside the White House, calling out to the president each time he came or left. They marched in parades in cities and towns across the country.

Success at Last

20 Finally, in 1919, Congress passed the Nineteenth Amendment to the Constitution. This is how it reads:

21   The right of citizens of the United States to vote shall not be denied or abridged by the United States or by any State on account of sex.

22   By the end of August 1920, two-thirds of the states had approved the amendment. It became the law of the land.

23   The election of November 1920 made history. For the first time, and in every state, women were allowed to cast votes. The right they had been denied for so long was finally theirs.

Questions

1. What happened in Seneca Falls, New York in 1848?

2. What was the most important thing the women wanted?

3. What did women base their right to vote on?

4. When did Congress pass the Nineteenth Amendment?

Identifying Cause and Effect/ Summarizing and Paraphrasing

1. Why did some women, Susan B. Anthony among them, vote in the election of 1872?

2. Why did the suffragists begin to focus their attention on changing the Constitution?

3. Write a summary of the section "Call to Action."

4. Paraphrase, or state in your own words, what the Nineteenth Amendment says.

Ready for High Speeds

What does it take to be a race car driver? Are driving skills enough, or is there more to it than that?

1 The track at the Indianapolis 500 Speedway is 2 1/2 miles long. At speeds of about 250 miles per hour, you can whip around the track in about 38 seconds. You make a left turn, then drive a short straight stretch. After another left turn, there's another straight run, then you must turn left again. The track is packed with other cars. At any moment, a car could cut in front of you and crash into the wall. Or you could crash. You make another left turn and go into the straight!

2 Then you do it all again—199 more times—as fast as you can push your car.

Staying Calm

3 What kind of a person do you have to be to drive a race car? One thing you need is nerve—and plenty of it. At 250 miles per hour, a crash is never more than a split second away. You're driving a car that's being pushed to the limit. The engine is turning 10,000 times per

minute, hour after hour. Most cars used for street driving would blow up if pushed past 7,000 turns per minute. The wheels, the clutch, or any part of the car could let go at any moment. But you stay calm and dive into the next turn.

4   The human heart beats about 75 times per minute. During a race, a driver's heartbeat jumps up to 160, even 180! At the Indianapolis 500, a driver gets a bit of a break during a yellow flag. That's when the track is cleared after a crash. But in races like the Grand Prix [pree], a driver's heart hammers at 180 beats per minute nonstop for two hours!

No Rest

5   Most people would feel completely exhausted. But you can't rest during a race. Race car drivers have to train their bodies. Formula 1 drivers' average heart rate while resting is down around 63 beats per minute. Their bodies also make better use of the oxygen they breathe. This means that even at their high heart rate during a race, drivers still have energy left at the end of races. And they may need it if their cars' steering starts to wear out.

Good Shape

6   Drivers also have to be in good shape. Body fat takes blood away from the brain and muscles. It also keeps the body warm. In a hot race car, an overweight person would feel too warm. Drivers also need to be able to bend their bodies easily. They will less likely be hurt in a crash if their bodies can bend.

7   Good eyes are another "must." Drivers have to see things that are far away and be able to quickly judge how far away they are. They also have to see close-up things, like the oil gauge. Drivers also must be able to see things clearly out of the corners of their eyes. Drivers need this kind of vision to see, for example, a wheel come off the car to the right.

Reaction Time

8 Seeing objects ahead of time isn't enough. A driver has to decide what to do about what he or she sees—and do it—in an instant. How fast a person can act is called *reaction time*. Anyone who drives a car needs good reaction time, but in a race, a driver has to think much faster. Even one-hundredth of a second can make a huge difference. At 200 miles per hour, that split second equals a whole car length!

9 A driver can test his or her reaction time on a machine. On the machine, eight buttons are set into a desktop shaped in a half circle. The driver has to hit the buttons that light up, one after the other. The buttons are wired to a computer, which counts the driver's reaction time. Indianapolis 500 drivers are very quick. Formula 1 drivers, who must race on turning, twisting roads, are even quicker.

Mario Andretti

10 Drivers have to be able to concentrate on the race— and keep on concentrating. They can never let up. Mario Andretti [an•dreh´•tee] wrote about the first time he won the Indianapolis 500, in 1969. By the 110th lap, he was a whole lap ahead of all the other cars on the track. All he had to do was keep his car on the track for 90 more laps, and he would win. But twice he almost lost it. First, on the 150th lap, he was thinking about everything except what he was doing. He got too close behind another car. Caught in its draft, he flipped sideways and found himself headed straight for the wall.

11 The second time, toward the end of the race, Andretti forgot for a moment what he was doing. At 200 miles per hour, a moment is a long time! Again he almost drove into the wall. After that, he said, he kept his head—and won the race.

A Good Attitude

12 One more thing race car drivers need is a good attitude. They have to go into races with the idea that they're going to win. Some drivers do this by thinking back to times they have felt the best, the most ready, and the most confident. They set their minds to feel the same way again. They take time before a race to get their minds ready for racing.

13   When you think about it, these sound like good tips for succeeding at just about anything. Stay calm. Concentrate. Think fast. Keep an eye on everything that's happening around you. Keep your body in good shape. And whatever you do, keep a good attitude. With all this going for you, how could you lose?

14   One more thought comes from Grand Prix winner Jacky Ickx [iks]. He says that his greatest races were not always the races he won. They were ones in which he felt a personal triumph. The real winning is inside yourself.

Questions

1. How long is the track at the Indianapolis Speedway?

2. Why is it important for a race car driver to be good shape?

3. What happened to Mario Andretti when he didn't keep his mind on driving?

4. In what year did Mario Andretti win his first Indianapolis 500 race?

Summarizing and Paraphrasing/Supporting Evidence

1. Paraphrase, or state in your own words, why the author thinks race car drivers should have a good attitude.

2. Write a summary of the section "Staying Calm."

3. Find evidence that supports the idea that reaction time is important for a race car driver.

The Trade-Off

How did tenants of a San Francisco apartment building help turn a dangerous place to live into a safe one?

1 Geneva Towers was the most dangerous housing project in San Francisco. Gangs shot at one another. When the police came, the gangs threw garbage at them. The police were pinned down by sniper fire.

2   Not anymore. Geneva Towers is clean of drug traffic, gangs, crime, and even graffiti [gruh•fee´•tee]. The story of how this happened shows us some things.

3   First, a dangerous housing project *can* be made safe. But it takes a lot of force. Second, the price is high in two ways. It costs a lot of money. And people must sacrifice some freedom to be rid of fear.

Taking Over

4 The story began on June 6, 1991. That day, a federal government agency took over Geneva Towers. The agency was the Department of Housing and Urban Development (HUD). It had decided that the two buildings were unsafe.

5   HUD hired the John Stewart Company to run the buildings. The John Stewart Company had turned around small housing projects before. But it had never worked in one as big as Geneva Towers. Each of the two buildings has 19 floors. Together there are 576 apartments. Eight hundred people live there.

6   Mari Tustin works for the John Stewart Company. The plan for Geneva Towers was simple. She said, "You secure it, and you clean it up. And you do it instantly."

Garbage and Gangs

7 The cleanup job at Geneva Towers was huge. Heaps of garbage and broken glass filled the lawns. Graffiti covered every wall, and most of the windows were boarded up. The garages were filled with abandoned cars. Gang members hid their guns and drugs in the cars.

8   When workers came to clean up, about 50 residents helped. They took away 90 trash bins of junk. They towed away more than 100 cars. They put in new windows and steamed the graffiti off the walls. But keeping the graffiti off the walls turned into a war. The workers would clean the walls during the day. And at night, the gangs would sneak back again. This went on for months. Finally, the gangs got bored and stopped.

9   Getting rid of the gangs caused another war. The gangs ran every floor in both buildings. They ran the garages, the lobbies, and even the sidewalks. The John Stewart Company hired a private security company. They sent Eli Gray to deal with the gangs. Gray had been a casino bouncer in Las Vegas.

The Crackdown

10 Geneva Towers had 15 guards, who were paid the minimum wage. Only one shift out of three had guns. Gray heard that some guards sold drugs in the building. So he fired most of them. He then hired 60 new guards and paid them more. They all have

uniforms. They also have guns, nightsticks, and spray cans of Mace. They wear bulletproof vests.

11   Gray made other changes. All tenants now enter each building through one room. If the guards don't know them, they must identify themselves. All guests must sign in.

12   The security company put zoom cameras on the roofs, in the parking lots, and in the halls and lobbies. The cameras send the pictures to a main dispatch room with six viewing screens.

13   A 10-foot fence was built around Geneva Towers. Bright light now floods the halls and outdoors. Buzzers were placed on all the fire exits. If a door opens, it rings in the dispatch room. This tells the guards to watch the screens.

Private vs. Public

14 Geneva Towers is not a public housing project. It was built by a private company, not the government. This makes a big difference. The guards can do things the law says can't be done in public housing. For example, the guards evicted 70 troublemakers. That would be hard to do in public housing. Also, the guards think of themselves as private citizens. That gives them the right to make citizen's arrests. When they search suspicious [sus•spish´•uhs] visitors and find drugs or guns, they call the police.

15   How far can the guards go? The U.S. Constitution protects people against unlawful search and seizure. Gray says this applies only to search and seizure done by government workers, such as the police. He says it does not apply to search and seizure done by private citizens, like the guards at Geneva Towers.

Lease Conditions

16 The guards enter apartments if they think there is an emergency. It might be a tip on drug use. It could be a

neighbor complaining. Or it could be something suspicious the guards see on the cameras. The police usually can't enter and search a home without a warrant. An exception to this rule is if police are in "hot pursuit" of a suspect. Another is if the police hear the sound of screams or gunfire.

17   Why can the guards enter apartments in an "emergency" without permission? Each tenant's lease is written this way. The lease also says that the landlords can make nonemergency visits, with permission, during reasonable hours. This might be to make repairs inside an apartment.

18   The law is not clear about how far the guards can go. It does state that citizens may not bother or assault other citizens. This would apply also to the guards. But many other housing projects want to try the plan used at Geneva Towers. And they probably can.

Worth the Price

19 Dorothy Dean is 70 years old. She has lived in Geneva Towers for 27 years. She says, "It was just like a jungle. The security they got now, I'm so pleased. If they got rid of the security here, I'd be ready to leave." The car of Cornelia Simpo, another resident, was broken into twice. Now Simpo feels safe. She says the guards "had to rough a few people up, but I don't see any harm in that."

20   Other residents think the guards go too far at times. They have complained. But Gray says that the guards do what they must to make the project safe. The first year after the guards came, crime dropped. The number of shootings fell from 33 to 7. Violent assaults fell from 66 to 7. In the next year, no major crime was reported in Geneva Towers.

21   Most of the tenants say they are glad to finally have peace and security. They think it is worth giving up some freedom to be safe.

Questions

1. Which agency took control of Geneva Towers?
2. Why did Eli Gray fire most of the original guards at Geneva Towers?
3. List two of the changes Eli Gray made to the management of Geneva Towers.
4. Why can the guards enter a tenant's apartment without permission?

Predicting Outcomes/Identifying Fact and Opinion

1. Write a paragraph predicting what would happen if a plan similar to the Geneva Plan was used on a city-wide level.
2. Do you think the guards at Geneva Towers abused the search and seizure protection guaranteed by the U.S. Constitution? Why or why not?
3. Do you think the benefits the people who live in Geneva Terrace receive are greater than the sacrifices in personal freedom they make? Why or why not?

The Art of Acupuncture

What is acupuncture? Can it ease pain and cure disease?

1   For more than 2000 years, the Chinese have used acupuncture [ak´•yoo•pungk•chur] to treat health problems. They use it to ease pain, treat arthritis, and cure other ailments. They even use it to treat deafness. The Chinese and other Asians still use acupuncture today.

2   Most Westerners know little about acupuncture. Yet acupuncture is growing more and more popular in the United States. Doctors who research this ancient healing art want to find out how it works. They want to know *why* it works.

An Ancient Art

3   Acupuncturists stick needles into a person's skin. They use very thin needles. Usually, they insert the needles just a fraction of an inch into the skin.

4   Acupuncturists carefully place each needle in a precise spot. There are more than 500 such spots, called *points,* on the human body. Acupuncturists place

needles in different points, depending on the ailment they treat. For instance, they may insert needles in 40 different points. Or they may use only one point.

5   How does the practice work? First, experts insert the needles. Then they move the needles gently. In ancient days, they twirled the needles by hand. Some experts use this method today. Others heat up the needles. Still others send a weak electric current through the needles.

6   Acupuncturists say that the moving needles block pain. The needles, they claim, can control blood pressure and can help addicts withdraw from alcohol and drugs. They can also control appetite and relieve asthma [az´•muh].

Pain-Free Surgery

7 Western doctors are starting to believe that some of these claims have value. One study compared two groups of stroke victims. The first group got regular therapy. The other group got regular therapy *plus* acupuncture. The second group made a faster and more complete recovery.

8   The Chinese point to even stronger proof. Chinese doctors often use acupuncture during surgery in place of anesthetics [an•ihs•theht´•iks]. Acupuncture, they say, works better than drugs. Patients stay alert—but pain free—during surgery. There are no side effects, and the patients recover quickly. Acupuncture also costs much less than drugs.

9   In China, doctors use acupuncture for nearly one-third of all surgeries. They often use it for both minor and major operations. Doctors have used acupuncture for surgery on the heart, lungs, eyes, kidneys, and brain.

10   There is a downside. On some people, acupuncture does not work. On others, the effect may wear off during long operations. Still other patients feel painful tugs or pulls.

11   Even so, acupuncture has gained much support in the United States. About 9000 acupuncture professionals hold millions of sessions about the method each year. Some patients turn to these doctors when mainstream treatment fails. Others believe that the body can be stirred to heal itself.

An Ancient Theory

12   How does acupuncture affect the body? How does it block pain? According to ancient Chinese theory, the human body contains a strong life force or *ch'i* [chee]. This force controls the body's organs. It provides the energy that makes the body work. The energy travels through the body along set paths. Sometimes the energy flow is disrupted and gets out of balance. This imbalance causes pain and disease.

13   To ease pain or cure disease, *ch'i* must be restored, and balance must be returned. Doctors who use acupuncture place needles at certain points along the energy paths. The needles stimulate the energy flow. The Chinese say that such movement restores *ch'i* and, in turn, the health of both body and mind.

Western Theories

14   Many Western doctors agree that acupuncture eases pain. But they have different theories to explain why. One theory involves the body's natural painkillers. Doctors have found chemicals in the body that kill pain. Perhaps acupuncturists already knew the places in the body where the needles could trigger the natural painkillers.

15   A second theory has to do with how the brain senses pain. When a part of the body gets hurt, it sends a message to special pain receptors. These receptors, found in the brain and spinal cord, get a pain message. They send it on to tell the body that it feels pain. A

person says "ouch!" only after the receptors send a pain message.

16 Some doctors think that acupuncture needles can turn off these pain receptors. They think that the needles cause a burst of messages. These messages flood the receptors and cause an overload. Because the receptors cannot send any pain messages, the patient feels no pain. When the needles are removed, the overload ends. The receptors can once again send pain messages.

Alternative Medicine

17 No one is sure why acupuncture works, but it has helped a large number of people. This treatment is part of a growing trend called alternative medicine. Alternative treatments use the body's ability to heal itself.

18 Alternative treatments vary widely. Prayer, music, and dance are some examples. Yoga, meditation, special breathing, herb therapy, and healing by touch are others.

19 Some alternative treatments are known as "folk" treatments. They seem old-fashioned, yet they often work. Today, many Western doctors use these treatments with their patients. Some people say that this is daring. But the Chinese probably say, "What took you so long?"

Questions

1. What do supporters of acupuncture say that this treatment can do?

2. How is acupuncture performed?

3. What proof do Chinese doctors give to show that acupuncture works?

4. What role do the Chinese believe *ch'i* plays in a person's health?

5. What two theories do Western doctors give to explain why acupuncture works?

Recognizing Author's Purpose/Recognizing Author's Point of View/Making Generalizations

1. What is the author's purpose for writing this article?

2. How would you describe the author's point of view on acupuncture? Is it positive, negative, or neutral? Give examples from the selection to support your answer.

3. After reading about acupuncture, what generalization, or general statement, can you make about alternative medicine?

NAFTA:
Boon or Bust?

What does the North American Free Trade Agreement mean for the United States' economy?

1 In 1993, Congress approved the North American Free Trade Agreement (NAFTA). The agreement went into effect on January 1, 1994. NAFTA was a hot topic then. And it has not cooled down much since. Some people love this trade pact, but others bitterly oppose it. Why has NAFTA stirred up so much trouble?

What Is NAFTA?

2 NAFTA is a kind of treaty—a written agreement between nations. It was signed by the United States, Canada, and Mexico. The goal of NAFTA was to make trade between these countries free. Free trade would lead to more trade and, therefore, benefit all three nations.

3   The three countries have always traded, or exchanged goods and services, with each other. But they all had barriers to free trade, mostly as import taxes, or tariffs. Most of the tariffs were between the United States and Mexico. For example, a U.S. tariff on

clothing made in Mexico added to the cost of Mexican-made clothing sold in the United States. So clothing made in Mexico was no cheaper for Americans to buy than U.S.-made clothing. The tariff, therefore, protected U.S. clothing makers, who have higher manufacturing costs than Mexican clothing makers.

4   In the same way, Mexico put a tariff on certain goods made in the United States. The tariff protected Mexican manufacturers: they can't make the same products as cheaply or as well as U.S. companies can.

5   Under NAFTA, the United States, Canada, and Mexico promised to get rid of these tariffs and other trade barriers. Factories in any of the three nations could make products and sell them anywhere from southern Mexico to northern Canada. Trade would be similar to that between, for example, New York and New Jersey. There is no import tax on goods exchanged between these states. There is no limit on what or how much can be traded, either. NAFTA would unite the three nations as one giant market of more than 360 million consumers. With so many more buyers and sellers of goods, more products would be made—and many jobs created. The treaty would increase trade, lower prices, and boost the economies of all three countries.

The Case Against NAFTA

6 The NAFTA issue caused heated debate between Democrats and Republicans. The people in the two parties disagree on most major issues. But when it came to NAFTA, many of them crossed party lines and took the same side.

7   Opponents of NAFTA focused on one point. The treaty, they said, would cost many Americans their jobs. The opponents believed that U.S. companies would move their factories to Mexico. Workers there earn much less money than those in the United States and

Canada. A company could save a lot of money by paying low wages to Mexican workers. As a result, NAFTA opponents believed, many Americans would lose their jobs to Mexican workers.

8   Opponents made another point. They worried that the United States would no longer be able to govern its own affairs. For example, they feared that the rules of the treaty would weaken U.S. pollution laws. The United States has strict laws to protect the country's land, air, and water. NAFTA opponents noted that Mexico's laws against pollution are less strict than U.S. laws. Many people feared that U.S. companies would move to Mexico to avoid the demanding U.S. laws.

The Case For NAFTA

9   NAFTA supporters agreed with opponents on one point. Some low-skill jobs *would* be lost. However, the supporters argued, such jobs would be lost anyway: in time, these low-skill jobs would go to people in low-wage countries such as China. Paul Tsongas [sahn´•gus], a well-known Democrat, was not worried about losing low-skill, low-wage jobs. He wrote, "I don't want to see Americans competing with Mexicans for low-wage jobs. I want to see [them] compete with Germans and Japanese for high-wage jobs." Tsongas's words pointed to yet a higher goal of NAFTA than the added jobs caused by free trade. NAFTA would increase trade between the United States, Canada, and Mexico. And such growth in business activity would, in time, lead to greater success for all three nations and a better life for their citizens.

10   Supporters said that NAFTA would create about 200,000 jobs in the United States. Free trade would result in millions of Canadian and Mexican buyers of U.S. products. So companies would hire plenty of workers to export goods and services to these countries.

11   NAFTA supporters also felt that a free-trade pact would especially help Mexico thrive. More and

higher-paying jobs would raise Mexico's standard of living. A higher standard of living would make it easier to sell U.S. goods in Mexico. In this way, NAFTA would make Mexico a more attractive place to live.

12   That, in turn, might reduce the number of illegal aliens who enter the United States. Many Mexicans slip across the border each year to find better jobs. If they could have good jobs in Mexico, there would be no need to leave.

The Result

13 The NAFTA debate raged for months. For a while, it looked as if the treaty would not pass. But in the end, Congress approved it. The vote in the House of Representatives was 234 to 200. Both Democrats and Republicans voted for the treaty. Without support from both parties, NAFTA would not have passed.

14   NAFTA's full effect on the business world is not yet known. Although jobs have been lost, the worst fears about NAFTA have not come to pass. Industry has created new jobs, but the greatest hopes for NAFTA have not been fulfilled, either. A true outcome of this historic trade pact will take about 20 years. Only then will the long-term effect of NAFTA show whether it was worth all the fuss.

Questions

1. What is the goal of the North American Free Trade Agreement?

2. Why was the political fight over NAFTA unusual?

3. What were some arguments both for and against NAFTA?

Identifying Fact and Opinion/Genre

1. Skim the selection and identify one fact and one opinion about NAFTA.

2. After reading the selection, do you think NAFTA will benefit the economy of the United States? Give reasons for your opinion.

3. In what kind of publication might you find this selection about NAFTA? Why?

A Tarantula—
Big
Hairy
Deal

Are tarantulas really as dangerous as they look?

1   Tarantulas [tuh•ran´•chuh•luhz] are the largest spiders on Earth. Some of them grow to be the size of a person's hand. A few get even bigger than that. The largest ones can be the size of a dinner plate.

2   Maybe it's their size that makes tarantulas so scary. Or maybe it's their hairy bodies. Their eight beady eyes do nothing to calm the nerves, either. Then there are those two large fangs filled with venom [ven´•uhm]. All in all, tarantulas look quite fearsome, so they have been portrayed as aggressive killers. In movies and on TV, tarantulas have long been a symbol of death. Certain folklore may also play a part in the "bad rap" these creatures have had to live with through the ages.

3   The word *tarantula* comes from a large spider found near Taranto, a city in southern Italy. People once thought that a bite from this spider caused a sickness called *tarantism* [tar´•uhn•tiz•uhm]. People with this illness were said to leap into the air and run wildly, making odd noises. The best cure in that day was a

lively folk dance. The dance became known as the *tarantella,* which is still performed today—but not to cure disease!

Interesting But Not Deadly

4 The truth about tarantulas is less frightening than the myths of old would have you think. Tarantulas *do* kill with their venom, but they don't kill humans. Their venom is designed mostly for beetles and grasshoppers. It can't disable anything larger than a mouse or bat. Tarantulas rarely bite humans. When they do, the bite is no worse than a wasp sting.

5 Although tarantulas do not hunt humans, they are still fascinating. Scientists have found about 800 kinds, which live mostly in warm climates. They live in the American Southwest, Europe, and Asia. In fact, they live on every continent but Antarctica. Many tarantulas make their homes in rain forests. Scientists think that these forests hold many unknown species of tarantulas.

As Blind as a . . . Tarantula?

6 All tarantulas share certain features. They have long, hairy legs and thick, hairy bodies. Despite their many eyes, tarantulas do not see well. In this case, more is not better. Tarantulas must rely on other senses to help them get what they need.

7 Most important of these is the spiders' sense of touch. Tarantulas travel by feeling their way along. They find prey by picking up vibrations made by the prey as it moves. All the hairs on the tarantulas' bodies help them sense these vibrations. The hairs move with even the slightest breeze. So when their hairs start vibrating, tarantulas know the air is swirling. That motion usually signals something nearby: dinner is on the way.

8 Tarantulas use one other trick as well. They spin silk threads near their burrows. If a creature hits one of these threads, the thread jiggles. The jiggling alerts the tarantula that food is nearby.

A Liquid Diet

9   A tarantula hunts for food at night. Once it finds its prey, the spider moves fast. It sinks its fangs deep into the victim's body, paralyzing it with venom. Then the tarantula can take its time. It often drags its prey back to its burrow or to some other safe place. Then it does something odd. Since a tarantula cannot eat solid foot, it pumps digestive [die•jes´•tiv] fluids onto its victim. These fluids, which look like many wet threads of silk, come from silk glands at the rear of the spider. The silken juices cover the victim and wrap around it. Soon the flesh of the victim dissolves into liquid. The spider then sucks out the liquids from the victim. Feeding can go on for hours, until nothing is left of the victim but a dry husk.

10   In the winter, tarantulas hibernate. In the summer, they eat only about once a week. If they must, they can go much longer than that without a meal. One large female was kept away from food for a long time. After two years, she was still alive.

The Hunter Is Hunted

11   Tarantulas eat many small creatures but may themselves be eaten by other animals. Their worst enemy is the female Pepsis wasp. The Pepsis is a big wasp—the largest in the world. Because of its size and diet, it is nicknamed the "tarantula hawk."

12   Although large for a wasp, the Pepsis is still smaller than a tarantula. Sometimes it is much, much smaller. A tarantula may weigh 10 times as much as a Pepsis, but that doesn't stop a fighting wasp. She will swoop down and try to sting a tarantula at the base of a leg. The tarantula, meanwhile, tries to bite the wasp. The battle can be fierce, and the stakes are high. The loser, after all, ends up dead.

13   If the wasp wins, she lays a single egg on top of the dead tarantula. Then she buries the spider. When the egg hatches, the baby wasp finds itself sitting on its first meal!

Self-Defense

14 Tarantulas have several ways to protect themselves from wasps and other enemies. One defense they use is a loud hissing sound to scare enemies away. Tarantulas make the hissing noise by rubbing their legs together. The spider's leg hairs produce the sound.

15 Hair also plays a role in a second defense. When threatened, tarantulas rub their back legs over their bellies, rubbing off many hairs. These hairs fly through the air, and some may hit the enemy. They cause a strong burning or itching feeling on the enemy's skin. Mice that inhale these hairs have died from their effects.

16 A tarantula has a third and final defense. As a last resort, it will use its huge fangs to bite an attacker that tries to get away.

Popular Pets

17 Some people say that the more they learn about tarantulas, the more they like them. That may be why tarantulas are popular in pet stores. More and more people are buying them. Owners praise tarantulas as wonderful pets. Tarantulas don't bark like dogs, eat a lot, smell, make messes, or take up much room. And they are quite interesting to watch.

18 Even so, it is hard to shake the old image of tarantulas as symbols of terror. Their place on the Halloween scene ranks with the likes of vampires and rattling skeletons. So if the thought of a tarantula on the loose makes you cringe, you're not alone. Just remember that a tarantula's "bark" is far worse than its bite!

Questions

1. How did tarantulas get their name?
2. How does a tarantula find food?
3. How does a Pepsis wasp act toward a tarantula?
4. Name three ways a tarantula can defend itself from enemies.

Identifying Genre and Style Techniques/Recognizing Author's Effect and Intention/Applying Passage Elements

1. Would this selection be more likely to appear in a science textbook or a general-interest magazine? Explain your choice.
2. What technique does the author use the most to help readers visualize tarantulas—word choice, imagery, figurative language, personification? Give examples to support your answer.
3. Describe the author's tone in this selection. Identify sentences that you think are particularly good examples of this tone.
4. Why don't tarantulas live in Antarctica?
5. Why do some people think that tarantulas make good pets?

Strange Case of Dr. Jekyll and Mr. Hyde

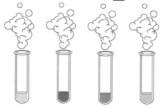

adapted from Robert Louis Stevenson

Robert Louis Stevenson wrote essays, poetry, and travel books. He is best known for his many adventure novels that always present moral conflicts.

Story of the Door

1 Mr. Utterson the lawyer seldom spoke and rarely smiled. He was lean, long, dusty, dreary—and yet somehow lovable. It was his way not to judge others. And when a friend went wrong, it was Mr. Utterson's habit to help rather than to lecture.

2 His friends were those of his own blood or those he had known the longest, and that would explain the bond that linked him with Richard Enfield, his distant cousin. Mr. Enfield was the well-known man about town. It was a nut to crack for many, what these two men could see in each other. Yet every week the two of them could be seen taking their Sunday walk together. And it was said that the two men regarded these outings as the chief jewel of each week.

3   It so happened that one of these rambles led them down a side street in a busy part of London. It was a pretty street, and well kept up. Except, that is, for one house. It was two stories high with no windows and nothing but a door on the lower story. The door had neither bell nor knocker. Its paint was blistered and discolored.

4   Mr. Enfield and the lawyer were on the other side of the street. As they passed, Enfield lifted up his cane and pointed.

5   "Did you ever notice that door?" he asked his kinsman. "It is connected in my mind with a very odd story."

6   "Indeed?" said Mr. Utterson, with a slight change of voice. "And what was that?"

7   "Well, it was this way," replied Mr. Enfield. "I was coming home about three o'clock of a black winter morning, and all at once I saw two figures. One was a man who was stumping along at a good clip, and the other was a girl of maybe eight or ten who was running as hard as she was able. Well, sir, the two ran into one another at the corner. Then came the horrible part. The man trampled calmly over the child's body and left her screaming on the ground.

8   "It sounds like nothing to hear, but it was hellish to see. I took to my heels and collared the man, and brought him back. There was already quite a group around the screaming child. He gave me one look, so ugly that it brought out the sweat on me.

9   "Well, the child was more scared than hurt. But I had taken a violent dislike to that man at first sight. And so had the crowd. I never saw such a circle of hateful faces. And there was the man in the middle, with a kind of black, sneering coolness.

10   "The man decided to buy his way out. 'Name your figure,' said he. Well, we insisted on a hundred pounds for the child's family. And the next thing was to get the

money. And where do you think he led us but to that door across the street! He gave us a check signed with a name I can't mention. But it's a name very well known and highly regarded."

11   "Tut-tut," said Mr. Utterson.

12   "Yes," agreed Mr. Enfield, "it's a bad story. For my man was a fellow that nobody could have anything to do with. And the person who signed that check is one of those fellows who do what you call good. Blackmail, I suppose. So 'Blackmail House' is what I call that place."

13   "If I were you," said the lawyer, "I would keep the story to myself. But for all that, there's one point I want to ask. I want to ask the name of that man who walked over the child."

14   "Well," said Mr. Enfield, "I can't see what harm it would do. It was a man by the name of Hyde."

15   "Hmm," said Mr. Utterson. "What sort of a man is he to look at?"

16   "He is not easy to describe. I never saw a man I so disliked, and yet I hardly know why. He is not deformed. But there is something wrong with his appearance—something downright detestable!"

17   Mr. Utterson mulled over his reply and they walked some way in silence.

18   "If I do not ask you the name of the other man," said Utterson out of the blue, "it is because I know it already!" Mr. Utterson sighed deeply.

19   "Let us make a bargain," said the young man, "never to refer to this again."

20   "With all my heart," said the lawyer. "I shake hands on that, Richard."

Search for Mr. Hyde

21 That evening after dinner, Mr. Utterson opened his safe. He took out an envelope that said on it, "Dr. Jekyll's Will." He sat down with a clouded brow to study its

contents. It said that "In case of the death of Henry Jekyll, all that he owns is to pass into the hands of his friend, Edward Hyde." And not only that. "In case of Dr. Jekyll's disappearance, the said Edward Hyde should step into the said Henry Jekyll's shoes without delay!"

22   This will had long been the lawyer's eyesore. It was bad enough when the name Hyde was just a name. Now it was even worse. "I thought it was madness," said Utterson to himself. "Now I begin to fear it is disgrace."

23   With that he blew out his candle, put on a greatcoat, and went out to visit Dr. Lanyon. "If anyone knows, it will be Lanyon," he thought.

24   "I suppose, Lanyon," he stated later that evening, "you and I must be the two oldest friends that Henry Jekyll has?"

25   "I wish the friends were younger," chuckled Dr. Lanyon. "But yes, I suppose we are. And what of that? I see little of him now."

26   "Did you ever come across a friend of his by the name of Hyde?" asked Utterson.

27   "Hyde?" repeated Lanyon. "No. I never heard of him."

28   The lawyer left it at that. But from that night on, Utterson felt he had to see this man Hyde for himself. He began to haunt the door his kinsman had pointed out. "If he be Mr. Hyde," decided Utterson, "I shall be Mr. Seek!"

29   And at last his patience was rewarded. It was ten o'clock one night when Mr. Utterson heard an odd, light footstep drawing near. The lawyer could soon see what kind of man he had to deal with. Something about him, even at that distance, made Mr. Utterson shudder.

30   The man made straight for the door. As he came, he drew a key from his pocket.

31   Mr. Utterson stepped out and touched him on the shoulder as he passed. "Mr. Hyde, I think?"

32   Hyde shrank back with a hissing intake of breath. "That is my name. What do you want?"

33   "I am an old friend of Dr. Jekyll's. I thought the three of us might visit."

34   "I'm afraid that is impossible," replied Mr. Hyde, inserting the key. And then suddenly, "How did you know me?"

35   "We have common friends," said Mr. Utterson.

36   "Common friends?" echoed Mr. Hyde. "Who are they?"

37   "Jekyll, for instance," said the lawyer.

38   "He never told you!" cried Mr. Hyde with a flush of anger. And the next moment he had unlocked the door and disappeared inside.

39   The lawyer stood a moment where Mr. Hyde had left him. "God bless me," he said to himself, "the man seems hardly human! Oh, my poor old Henry Jekyll! If ever I read Satan's signature upon a face, it is on that of your new friend."

40   Around the corner there was a square of old, handsome houses. The house second from the corner belonged to Dr. Henry Jekyll. The old door used by Mr. Hyde was actually the back entrance to Dr. Jekyll's lab!

41   Mr. Utterson walked around the corner and knocked on the front door of his old friend's home. Jekyll's butler answered the knock.

42   "Is Dr. Jekyll at home, Poole?" asked the lawyer.

43   "I will see, Mr. Utterson," said Poole. "Will you wait here by the fire, sir?"

44   "Thank you," said the lawyer.

45   Poole was back shortly to say that Dr. Jekyll was gone out.

46   "I saw Mr. Hyde go in by the back door—the door to the lab, Poole," said Utterson. "Is that right, when Dr. Jekyll is away from home?"

47   "Quite right, Mr. Utterson, sir," answered the servant. "Mr. Hyde has a key."

48   "You mean he comes and goes as he pleases?"

49   "Yes, sir," said Poole. "And we all have orders to obey him."

50   "Hmm. Well, good night, Poole."

51   "Good night, Mr. Utterson."

52   And the lawyer set out homeward with a very heavy heart. In his mind's eye he saw, once more, the strange terms of the will.

Dr. Jekyll Was Quite at Ease

53   Two weeks later, Dr. Jekyll gave one of his pleasant dinners for five or six old cronies. Mr. Utterson stayed behind after the others had left.

54   "I have been wanting to speak to you, Jekyll," he began. "It's about that will of yours."

55   "My poor Utterson," replied the doctor with a bit of a smile. "I never saw a man so distressed as you were by my will."

56   "You know I never approved of it. And lately," continued the lawyer, "I have been hearing something of young Hyde."

57   The large handsome face of Dr. Jekyll grew pale. "I do not care to hear more," said he.

58   "What I heard was disgraceful," said Utterson.

59   "It can make no difference. You do not understand the position I am in, Utterson."

60   "Jekyll," said Utterson, "you know me. I am a man to be trusted. If you are being blackmailed, tell me! I have no doubt I can get you out of it."

61   "My good Utterson," said the doctor, "I would trust you before any man alive, if I could. But it isn't what you think. It is not so bad as that. And just to put your good heart at rest, I will tell you one thing. The moment I choose, I can be rid of Mr. Hyde. I beg of you, Utterson—let this matter sleep."

62   "I have no doubt you are right," said Utterson at last, getting to his feet.

63   Once again, Mr. Utterson started homeward with a heavy heart.

The Carew Murder Case

64 Nearly a year later, all of London was stunned by a hideous crime. A maid had gone upstairs to bed about eleven. It seems she sat down at the window, daydreaming. As she sat she saw a gentleman with white hair coming down the lane below her. Coming towards him was another gentleman. The two met just under the maid's window. The older man bowed and spoke; she couldn't make out just what.

65 The other man, she could see, was a certain Mr. Hyde who had once visited her master. He had in his hand a heavy cane. All of a sudden, Hyde broke out in a great flame of anger, stamping with his foot and waving his cane about. "Like a madman," the maid said. The old gentleman took a step back, and at that Mr. Hyde clubbed him to the ground. The next moment he was trampling his victim underfoot. She could hear the old gent's bones shatter, the girl said later.

66 By the time the police arrived, the murderer was long gone. But one splintered half of his cane had rolled into the gutter. It was of some rare and very heavy wood. An envelope was found upon the victim which bore the name and address of a Mr. Utterson.

67 This was brought to the lawyer the next morning. Utterson hurried to the police station where the body had been taken.

68 "Yes," said he, "I know him. I am sorry to say that this is Sir Danvers Carew!"

69 "Good God, sir!" exclaimed the officer. "Is it possible? It was a Mr. Hyde did it," he said. Then he brought out the broken cane.

70 Mr. Utterson went pale at the name of Hyde. The sight of the stick was a second blow. It was none other than the one he had himself presented to Henry Jekyll many years before! The lawyer decided to keep this fact to himself for the time being.

71   It was late that same day when Mr. Utterson arrived at Dr. Jekyll's door. Poole led him at once to the doctor's lab. A fire burned in the grate. There, close up to the warmth, sat Dr. Jekyll, looking deadly sick. He held out a cold hand, and greeted his old friend in a changed voice.

72   "Now," said Utterson, as soon as Poole had left them. "You have heard about the murder?"

73   The doctor shuddered. "They were shouting it in the streets," he said. "I heard them in my dining room."

74   "You have not been mad enough to conceal this fellow Hyde?"

75   "Utterson, I swear to God," cried the doctor. "I will never set eyes on him again! I am done with him in this world. It is all at an end. Mark my words, he will never more be heard of!"

76   The lawyer listened gloomily. "You seem pretty sure of him," said he. "And for your sake, I hope you are right. And now one word more. It was Hyde who was behind that will of yours?"

77   The doctor shut his mouth tight and nodded.

78   "I knew it," said Utterson. "He meant to murder you. You have had a narrow escape."

79   "I have had a lesson," returned Jekyll. "Oh, God, Utterson, what a lesson I have had!" And he covered his face for a moment with his hands.

80   Utterson let himself out. The newsboys, as he made his way home, were crying themselves hoarse in the streets. "Special edition! Shocking murder of Sir Danvers Carew!" Utterson had lost one dear friend and client. He could not help but wonder if he was about to lose another.

Remarkable Incident of Dr. Lanyon

81 Time ran on. Thousands of pounds were offered in reward, but Mr. Hyde had disappeared as though he had never existed.

82   A new life began for Dr. Jekyll. He entertained old friends; he went to church. He did good works. His face seemed to open and brighten. And for more than two months the doctor was at peace.

83   On the 8th of January, Utterson dined at the doctor's. But on the 12th and again on the 14th, the door was shut against the lawyer. "The doctor would see no one," said Poole.

84   Utterson decided to visit their old friend, Dr. Lanyon. There, at least, he was not turned away. But when he came in, he was shocked at the change in the doctor's appearance. The rosy man had grown pale. His flesh had fallen away. And there was a look in the eye suggesting some deep-seated terror of the mind.

85   "I have had a shock," Lanyon told his friend, "from which I shall never recover."

86   "Jekyll is ill also," observed Utterson. "Have you seen him?"

87   Lanyon's face changed. He held up a shaking hand. "I wish to see or hear no more of Dr. Jekyll! I am quite done with that person. I beg that you will never again mention one whom I regard as dead!"

88   "Tut-tut," said Mr. Utterson. And then, "Can't I do something? We are three very old friends, Lanyon. We shall not live to make others."

89   "Someday, Utterson, after I am dead, you may perhaps come to learn the whole story. In the meantime, if you can sit and talk with me of other things, for God's sake, stay and do so. But if you cannot steer clear of this cursed topic, then go, for I cannot hear it."

90   A week later Dr. Lanyon took to his bed. Within a month he was dead.

91   The night after the funeral, Utterson unlocked his safe. He drew from his pocket an envelope sealed with the seal of his old friend. On the outside of the envelope, in Lanyon's hand, was this: "PRIVATE: For the eyes of G.J. Utterson alone. Not to be opened until

the death or disappearance of Dr. Henry Jekyll." With a sigh, Utterson placed the packet in the inmost corner of his private safe.

The Last Night

92 Mr. Utterson was sitting by his fireside one evening when he was surprised by a visit from Poole, Dr. Jekyll's butler. He was extremely upset.

93 "Mr. Utterson," said the man, "there is something very wrong!"

94 "Now, take your time," said the lawyer, "and tell me what it is."

95 "You know the doctor's ways, sir," replied Poole. "How he shuts himself up. Well, he's shut up again in the lab. And Mr. Utterson, sir, I think there's been foul play!"

96 "Foul play!" cried the lawyer. "What do you mean?"

97 "I dare not guess, sir," was the answer. "But will you come along with me and see for yourself?"

98 Mr. Utterson's only answer was to rise and get his hat and greatcoat.

99 It was a wild cold night in March. The wind made talking difficult and flecked the blood into the face. The square, when they got there, was full of wind and dust. The thin trees in Dr. Jekyll's garden were lashing themselves along the railing.

100 "Now, sir," said Poole, "follow me as quietly as you can. I want you to hear, but I don't want you to be heard."

101 Mr. Utterson followed the butler to the door of the lab.

102 Poole knocked on the door. "Mr. Utterson, sir, asking to see you," he called.

103 A voice answered from within. "Tell him I cannot see anyone!"

104 Poole turned to Mr. Utterson. "Sir," he said, looking into the lawyer's eyes, "was that my master's voice?"

105   "It seems much changed," said the lawyer.

106   "Oh, sir," cried Poole, "do you think I do not know my master's voice after twenty years? No, sir, that is not Dr. Jekyll! It is my belief that there was murder done!"

107   "Poole," replied the lawyer, "I consider it my duty to break in that door!"

108   "Ah, Mr. Utterson, that is talking!" cried the butler.

109   Poole took up an ax for himself and handed Mr. Utterson an iron poker from the fireplace.

110   "Jekyll," cried Utterson in a loud voice, "I demand to see you!" He waited a moment, but there came no reply. "I give you fair warning: I must and shall see you—if not by fair means, then by foul! If not with your consent, then by brute force!"

111   "Utterson," said the voice, "for God's sake, have mercy!"

112   "Ah, that is not Jekyll's voice," cried Utterson. "It's Hyde's! Down with the door, Poole!"

113   Poole swung the ax over his shoulder. The door leaped against the lock and hinges. A dismal scream rang from the lab. Up went the ax again. Four times the blow fell. But the wood was tough and the door well made. It was not until the fifth blow that the lock burst. The wreck of the door fell inward upon the carpet.

114   The two men stood back a little and peered in. There on the floor lay the body of a man. They drew near on tiptoe. Turning the body over, they beheld the face of Edward Hyde! The cords of his face still twitched, but life was quite gone. The foul smell of a deadly drug hung in the air. Utterson knew that he was looking upon the body of a self-destroyer.

115   "We must have come too late," he said, "to save or to punish. It only remains for us to find the body of your master."

116   They searched the lab quickly, to no avail. Next, they turned to the doctor's desk. On it was a large

envelope bearing the name of Mr. Utterson. Inside was a short note in the doctor's handwriting, and dated at the top.

117   "Oh, Poole!" the lawyer cried. "He was alive and here this day! He cannot have disappeared in so short a space!"

118   "Why don't you read it, sir?" asked Poole.

119   "Because I fear," replied the lawyer. But he brought the paper to his eyes and read as follows.

120   My Dear Utterson,

121   When this shall fall into your hands, I shall have disappeared. Go, then, and read the letter which Lanyon warned me he would place in your keeping. And if you care to hear more, turn to the confession of

122   Your unworthy and unhappy friend,

123   Henry Jekyll

124   Attached was a sheaf of pages written in his old friend's hand. The lawyer put it in his pocket.

125   Turning to the butler he said, "It is now ten. I must go home and read these documents in private. But I shall be back before midnight. Then we shall send for the police."

126   Utterson trudged back to his office.

Dr. Lanyon's Story

127 This was the packet that the late Dr. Lanyon had left to Utterson upon his deathbed. It had been in the lawyer's safe now for some three months. His hands shaking, Utterson broke the seal on the envelope and began to read. This is what he read:

128   On the 9th of January, I received a note from our old friend Henry Jekyll. This is how it ran.

129   Dean Lanyon,

130   You are one of my oldest friends. There was never a day when I would not have given my right hand to help you. But now, it is your help I seek. Lanyon—my life, my honor, my reason, are all at your mercy. If you fail me tonight, I am lost!

131   Drive straight to my house. Poole, my butler, will be waiting for you with a certain drawer from my lab. This drawer I beg of you to carry back with you exactly as it is. At midnight, you will be visited by a man who will give his name as Hyde. Place the drawer in his hands.

132   Serve me, my dear Lanyon, and save

133   Your friend,
134   H.J.

135   Dr. Lanyon's story continued in this way:

136   I was certain that our old friend was insane. Still, I felt bound to do as he asked.

137   I left right away, got into a hansom, and drove straight to Jekyll's house. The butler was expecting me, just as the letter said. I took the drawer from his hands and returned home to wait.

138   The clock was just striking twelve when the knock sounded very gently on my front door. I opened the door myself.

139   "Are you come from Dr. Jekyll?" I asked.

140   He told me "Yes" and I bid him enter. Here, at last, I had a chance of clearly seeing this man Hyde. There was something abnormal and misbegotten about the creature that now faced me. I could not help but notice that my visitor was on fire with excitement.

141   "Have you got it?" he cried. "Have you got it?" He even laid his hand upon my arm and sought to shake me.

142   My blood seemed to run cold at his touch. "There it is," said I, pointing to the drawer.

143   He sprang to it. At the sight of its contents he uttered one loud sob of relief. As I watched, he measured out a few drops of a blood-red tincture from a small bottle. To this he added several grains of a white powder. The mixture, which was at first of a reddish hue, began to brighten in color. At the same time, it started to bubble and to throw off small fumes of vapor. Suddenly, the compound changed to a dark purple, then slowly faded to a watery green.

144   My visitor watched these changes with a keen eye. When they were complete, he put the glass to his lips and drank at one gulp. A cry followed. He reeled, staggered, clutched at the table, and held on. His face became suddenly black and the features seemed to melt and alter. The next moment I had sprung to my feet and leaped back against the wall.

145   "Oh, God!" I screamed, and "Oh, God!" again and again. For there before my eyes—pale and shaken, like a man restored from death—there stood Henry Jekyll!

146   I saw what I saw, and I heard what I heard, and my soul sickened at it. My life is shaken to its roots. Sleep has left me. The deadliest terror sits by me at all hours of the day and night. I feel that my days are numbered, and that I must die.

147   I will say but one thing, Utterson, and that will be more than enough. The creature who crept into my house that night was known by the name of Hyde, hunted in every corner of the land for the murder of Carew. But the man who left me in the early hours of the morning was none other than our old friend, Dr. Henry Jekyll!

Henry Jekyll's Full Statement of the Case

148   Here is what Dr. Jekyll wrote:

149   I have long believed that there are two sides to every human being. One part of him wants to do good

works and help his fellow man. The other part of him delights in doing evil. These two natures war within us, I saw. Most of us succeed in hiding this dreadful twin. But the prisons are full of criminals whose baser side has won out.

150   What if each, I wondered, could be housed in different bodies? Then the unjust might go his own way. And the more upright twin could devote his life to doing good.

151   Thus far my thinking had gone. And then one day in the lab I managed—quite by accident—to mix a strange drug. This compound had the power to separate the two personalities.

152   I purchased a large amount of a certain powder which I knew to be the crucial ingredient. Then late one night I mixed the potion. I watched as it boiled and smoked. And then, with a strong glow of courage, I drank of the potion.

153   The most racking pangs came over me. I felt a grinding in the bones, deadly nausea, and a feeling of horror. And then these pains lessened and I came to myself as if out of a great sickness. I felt younger, lighter, happier in body. I felt reckless, even wicked! The sensation delighted me like wine! I looked into the mirror. I saw for the first time Edward Hyde.

154   Evil was written broadly and plainly upon his face. And yet I felt no disgust. This, too, was myself.

155   Once more I prepared and drank the potion. Once more I suffered the pains of change. When next I looked in the mirror, I saw the face of the good Henry Jekyll.

156   I had but to drink the cup. With that simple act I could cast off the body of the well-known doctor and step into that of Edward Hyde! I smiled at the notion.

157   The next day I told my servants that a Mr. Hyde was to have the run of the house. And, of course, I drew up that will. If anything happened to Henry Jekyll, Edward Hyde could step into his shoes, his house, his money!

158   With these preparations completed, I began to enjoy my new self. When I look back upon Hyde's adventures, I admit I am shocked. Laws had no meaning for Hyde. They held no threat for him, either. Let him but escape into the lab. Give him a second or two to mix and swallow the potion. And whatever he had done, Edward Hyde would pass away like the stains of breath upon a mirror.

159   Some two months before the murder of Sir Danvers Carew, I had been out on one of my adventures. I returned at a late hour and shed the form of Hyde. I woke the next day in my bed with somewhat odd feelings. And then my eyes fell upon my hand. The hand of Henry Jekyll, as you know, is large, firm, white, and handsome. But the hand which I now saw was lean, corded, knuckly, and thickly shaded with hair. It was the hand of Edward Hyde!

160   I must have stared upon it for nearly half a minute. Then bounding from my bed, I rushed to the mirror. And at the sight of what met my eyes, my blood ran cold. Yes, I had gone to bed Henry Jekyll. But I had awakened Edward Hyde! I made my way quickly to the lab and downed the drink. Ten minutes later, Dr. Jekyll was sitting down to breakfast.

161   Small indeed was my appetite. Clearly, Edward Hyde was growing more powerful within me. It was becoming easier to throw off the body of the good doctor, and harder to regain it again. I was slowly losing hold of my better self.

162   The time had come to choose between the two. To cast in my lot with Jekyll was to give up the forbidden pleasures I had come to enjoy. To cast it in with Hyde was to become, once and for all, hated and friendless. I chose my better self. I wanted to die surrounded by friends, pursuing honest hopes.

163   For two months I stayed away from my lab. I devoted myself to good works. But soon Hyde was

struggling to come out. In an hour of weakness, I once again mixed and swallowed the drug.

164   The devil in me had long been caged. Now he came out roaring. That was the night Sir Danvers Carew bumped into me on the street. Instantly the spirit of hell awoke in me and raged. With a kind of glee, I clubbed the old man to the ground. I tasted delight with every blow. It was not until he was quite dead that I was struck through the heart by a cold thrill of terror. I fled from the scene and ran to the lab. Soon the form of Henry Jekyll had fallen upon his knees and lifted his clasped hands to God. Never again, I promised. And this time I meant to keep that promise.

165   From that day on, I was as good as my word. The days passed quietly, almost happily. I never dreamed of bringing back Hyde.

166   And then it happened again. It was on a fine, clear, January day in Regent's Park. I sat in the sun on a bench. I was smiling at the thought of my blameless life. And at that very moment the most deadly shuddering swept over me. It passed away and left me faint. The faintness too passed. I began to be aware of a change within my mind. Evil thoughts had replaced good. I looked down. The hand that lay on my knee was corded and hairy. I was once more Edward Hyde, a known murderer!

167   My drugs were in my lab. How was I to reach them? If I tried to enter through the house, my own servants would hand me over to the police. I thought of Lanyon. I remembered that one part of my old self remained to me: my handwriting. I wrote two letters, one to Lanyon and one to Poole. That night I visited Lanyon and quaffed the drug before his horrified eyes.

168   The next morning I was strolling in my own garden when, once again, it happened. I felt those terrible sensations come over me. I had barely made it into the lab before I was once again raging with the passions of

Hyde. This time I took a double dose to recover my old self. And alas! six hours after, as I sat looking sadly into the fire, the pangs returned. The drug had to be taken again. It was the beginning of the end.

169   At all hours of the day and night, I could feel it coming on. If I slept, or even dozed for a moment in my chair, it was always as Hyde that I awakened. I became a creature eaten up and emptied by fever. One thought alone occupied my mind: the horror of my other self. No one has ever suffered such torments.

170   My punishment might have gone on for years. But fate dealt me a final blow. My supply of the crucial powder began to run low. I sent out for a fresh batch and mixed the drink. It bubbled and changed color, as always. But the second color change failed to follow. I drank it, but it was without result.

171   I sent Poole all over London for more of the drug. It was in vain. I now believe that my first supply was impure. And it was this unknown impurity that makes the change.

172   About a week has passed. I am now finishing this statement under the influence of the last of the old powder. These, then, are the last words of Henry Jekyll. No more must I delay too long to bring my writing to an end. Should the throes of change take me in the act of writing it, Hyde will tear it to pieces.

173   This is my true hour of death. What is to follow concerns another than myself. Hyde's life too will soon come to an end. Whether on the gallows, or by his own hand, I cannot say.

174   Here, then, as I lay down the pen, I bring the life of that unhappy Henry Jekyll to an end.

Questions

1. To whom did Dr. Jekyll leave everything he owned in his will? Why did this bother his lawyer?

2. What did Edward Hyde do after the murder of Sir Danvers Carew?

3. What happened to Dr. Jekyll after the murder of Carew?

4. Mr. Utterson begged his old friend Jekyll to confide in him. What might have Utterson said or done if Jekyll had told him the whole story?

5. What did Mr. Utterson and Poole find when they broke into the lab?

6. How did Edward Hyde die?

7. Dr. Jekyll's body changed into Mr. Hyde's. How did his mind change?

8. Why do you think the good Dr. Jekyll could not stay away from his dangerous potion?

9. What do you think of Dr. Jekyll's theory? Would it be a good idea to separate our good side from our bad side? What, if anything, do we gain from our inner conflicts?

10. Which side won out in Dr. Jekyll—the good side or the evil side? Explain your answer.

Answer Key

America's Natural Wonders

Page 10: Questions
1. The National Park Service began in 1916.
2. Carlsbad Caverns are special because they contain some of the world's largest caves.
3. The Colorado River runs through the Grand Canyon.
4. Native American cliff dwellers, called the Anasazi, used to live in Mesa Verde.
5. "Old Faithful" is a geyser located in Yellowstone National Park.

Page 10: Synonym/Antonym Search
1. Paragraph 1: *consider*—When you *think* of national parks, most likely you think of mountains and lakes.
Paragraph 3: *created*—The National Park Service was *formed* in 1916.
Paragraph 5: *unbelievable*—Besides these *incredible* formations, on summer nights, visitors can watch thousands of bats fly out of a part of the cavern called the Bat Cave.
Paragraph 6: *investigate*—People who want to *explore* the park further can take a mule ride into the canyon.
Paragraph 8: *houses*—Some of the *dwellings* have more than 50 rooms and are two or three stories high.
2. Answers will vary.
3. Paragraph 2: Yosemite, Sequoia, and Mount Rainier were some of the *earliest.* Answers will vary.
Paragraph 5: The Carlsbad Caverns National Park in New Mexico is *unique.* Answers will vary.
Paragraph 6: Others can see the canyon in a *thrilling* raft ride down the Colorado River. Answers will vary.
Paragraph 11: Yosemite Valley is known for its *deep,* straight-walled canyon. Answers will vary.

Fiddler with a Smile

Page 15: Questions

1. Itzhak Perlman was ten years old when he first soloed with a major symphony orchestra.

2. Perlman has helped the causes of disabled people by serving on committees, by speaking to groups about the lack of handicapped facilities in hotels and public buildings, and by making people aware that disabled people want to be treated like everyone else.

3. Perlman was invited by Ed Sullivan to come and perform on national U.S. television.

4. A newspaper strike prevented a review of Perlman's Carnegie Hall debut.

Page 15: Using Context Clues

1. Perlman showed that he was a "determined" child by practicing walking with heavy braces after he was struck by polio.

2. A prodigy is a highly talented child or youth.

3. Perlman's career "took off like a meteor" through many live performances, recordings, television shows, and practice.

The Woman Behind the Lens

Page 19: Questions

1. Lange's decision to become a photographer was unusual because she had never taken a photograph or held a camera.

2. Lange gave up her studio work to go out in the real world and photograph "all kinds of people."

3. Lange photographed poor people and farm workers during the Great Depression.

4. This honor was unusual because it was the first time a woman photographer had her work shown.

Page 19: Spelling Word Alert
1. Paragraph 3: She hoped to take *photos* to help pay her way.
Paragraph 7: She took many photos of the awful working conditions in *factories*.
Paragraph 9: Two older *children* bury their faces in her shoulder.
Answers will vary.
2–4 Answers will vary.

Setting the Sky on Fire

Page 24: Questions
1. The color in fireworks is made by adding certain metal salts to them.
2. The sound of the blast comes after the light because sound doesn't travel as fast as light.
3. The way the shell is packed into the tube determines the shape of fireworks.
4. Fireworks are very dangerous to handle, so that is why there are tough laws about selling and using them.

Page 24: Recalling Details
1. The Chinese used fireworks more than 1000 years ago.
2. The "recipe" for making the black powder that goes into fireworks contains 75 parts saltpeter, 15 parts charcoal, and 20 parts sulfur.
3. Blue and purple are the colors that are the hardest to make.

The Birth of the Modern Olympics

Page 29: Questions
1. The first Olympic Games ended because they had become too professional, they had become corrupt, and the public had lost interest in them.

2. De Coubertin wanted to revive the games to promote peace among nations.
3. Answers will vary.
4. The IOC is the International Olympic Committee. Its purpose is to look after the growth and improvement of the Olympics.
5. Answers will vary.

Page 29: Identifying Sequence
1. The first modern Olympics were held four years after de Coubertin began his efforts to revive them.
2. The Olympic flag and oath were added before the first lighting of the Olympic flame.
3. The correct order is
1. Romans take over Greece.
2. The ancient Olympics come to an end.
3. The International Olympic Committee is formed.
4. Women begin to take part in the Olympics.
5. The first Winter Olympics are held.
6. Pierre de Coubertin dies.
7. The U.S.A. basketball Dream Team competes.

Habitat for Humanity
Page 34: Questions
1. Habitat for Humanity has been in existence for more than 20 years.
2. Habitat for Humanity keeps the cost of its houses down by seeking donations of money, land, and supplies.
3. They require that home buyers have some income, be able to pay back their loans within 20 years, and be willing to work as partners with Habitat for Humanity.
4. Former President Jimmy Carter and his wife are famous Americans involved with Habitat for Humanity.

Page 34: Recognizing Stated Concepts
1. The goal of Habitat for Humanity is to get rid of poverty-level housing and homelessness around the world.
2. It is part of a partnership by always working with the homeowners.
3. Answers will vary.

The World's Longest Railway

Page 39: Questions
1. Czar Alexander wanted a Trans-Siberian railroad to tie his vast land together.
2. Answers will vary.
3. Russian railroad builders faced dangers such as bad weather and attacks from Siberian tigers.
4. The trip across Siberia is boring because the area is a vast, empty plain with no variety in the scenery.
5. The Trans-Siberian railroad is important to Russia today because it has opened up Siberia to settlers, it has helped industry and mining, and it has become a lifeline between Siberia and European Russia.

Page 40: Using Maps and Graphs
1–3 Answers will vary.

Hong Kong: An Uncertain Future

Page 45: Questions
1. Great Britain won a war against China, and in a treaty signed after the war, was given ownership of Hong Kong.
2. Britain's control of the New Territories differed in that they did not own the New Territories but instead leased them.
3. Britain agreed with China, in 1984, that they would return Hong Kong to China in 1997.

4. This phrase means that even though Hong Kong is now part of China, it still has its own legal, social, and economic systems separate from China.

Page 45: Graphs/Dictionary
1. Answers will vary.
2. *Boom* can be a verb or a noun. The verb meaning of *boom* fits this sentence.
3. Answers will vary.

Cambodia's Grand Temple
Page 50: Questions
1. Hindu beliefs inspired the building of Angkor Wat.
2. Answers will vary.
3. The Khmer left Angkor Wat because armies from Thailand kept attacking, finally capturing Angkor in 1431.
4. Angkor has suffered damage through general neglect and theft.
5. Cambodians must decide whether to keep Angkor Wat as a holy shrine or to open it further to tourists.

Page 50: Dictionary/Index/Using Reference Sources
1–4 Answers will vary.

The Cold Facts
Page 55: Questions
1. A virus causes the common cold.
2. Cold sufferers should stop using nasal sprays or drops after three days because there could be a need for more and more of the product to keep the nose clear, as well as a risk of an increase in blood pressure.
3. A vaccine is helpful in preventing the flu but not a cold because there are far fewer flu viruses than cold viruses.
4. Answers will vary.

Page 55: Using Forms/Understanding Consumer Materials
1–2 Answers will vary.

Business Leader: Remedios Diaz-Oliver

Page 59: Questions
1. The future looked bright for Diaz-Oliver as a young girl because she was well traveled, she could speak several languages, and she was well educated.
2. Diaz-Oliver was jailed in 1961 because she protested the fact that Castro had people's mail checked.
3. The "E" stands for Excellence in Export.
4. In 1976 Diaz-Oliver, with her husband, started their own firm supplying glass and plastic bottles.

Page 59: Analyzing Character/Identifying Main Idea
1. She exhibited determination and perseverance in her early career at Emmer Glass.
2. Diaz-Oliver handled discrimination by remaing calm and using her good sense of humor. This shows that she could work well under pressure and wasn't forceful or rude.
3. The main idea of the selection is that Remedios Diaz-Oliver overcame adversity to become a sucessful business woman.

Faith, Family, and Farming

Page 65: Questions
1. The oldest Amish community in America is in Lancaster County in Pennsylvania.
2. The main kind of work the Amish do is farming.
3. The Amish use horse-drawn buggies for transportation.
4. Builders like to hire Amish workers because they are good carpenters who value hard work.

5. Some Amish couples have to move away because their families can't afford to buy them a farm and because the tourism demands can make their lives difficult.

Page 65: Comparing and Contrasting/Drawing Conclusions
1–5 Answers will vary.

Battle of the Ballot

Page 71: Questions
1. In 1848, 300 women met in Seneca Falls, New York to hold the first Women's Rights Convention.
2. The most important thing the women wanted was the right to vote.
3. Women based their right to vote on a new amendment, which in 1870 allowed male ex-slaves the right to vote.
4. Congress passed the Nineteenth Amendment in 1919.

Page 71: Identifying Cause and Effect/Summarizing and Paraphrasing
1. Some women voted in the 1872 election because they felt that the new amendment allowing male ex-slaves the right to vote applied to them as well.
2. The suffragists began to focus their attention on changing the Constitution because they felt that by adding an amendment they would get the right to vote.
3–4 Answers will vary.

Ready for High Speeds

Page 76: Questions
1. The track at the Indianapolis Speedway is 2½ miles long.
2. It is important for a race car driver to be in good shape to help him or her endure the rigors and dangers involved in racing a car.

3. Mario Andretti almost crashed twice when he didn't keep his mind in his driving.
4. Mario Andretti won his first Indianapolis 500 race in 1969.

Page 76: Summarizing and Paraphrasing/Supporting Evidence
1–3 Answers will vary.

The Trade-Off

Page 81: Questions
1. The Department of Housing and Urban Development took control of Geneva Towers.
2. Eli Gray fired most of the original guards because he had heard that some of them sold drugs in the building.
3. Answers will vary.
4. Guards can enter a tenant's apartment without permission because each lease is written that way.

Page 81: Predicting Outcomes/Identifying Fact and Opinion
1–3 Answers will vary.

The Art of Acupuncture

Page 86: Questions
1. Possible answer: Supporters of acupuncture say that this treatment can ease pain, treat arthritis, and control blood pressure.
2. Acupuncture is performed by inserting thin needles into a person's skin and moving the needles gently.
3. Chinese doctors have proof that acupuncture works because they have used this technique during major surgery.
4. *Ch'i* plays the role of keeping the energy flow in a person's body in balance thus keeping a person healthy.

5. Two theories that Western doctors give to explain why acupuncture works are 1. needles are inserted in certain areas that trigger natural painkillers and 2. the needles turn off pain receptors, so no pain messages are sent to the brain.

Page 86: Recognizing Author's Purpose/Recognizing Author's Point of View/Making Generalizations
1. The author's purpose for writing this article is to inform the reader about the art of acupuncture.
2–3 Answers will vary.

NAFTA: Boon or Bust?

Page 91: Questions
1. The goal of the North American Free Trade Agreement is to make trade free between the United States, Canada, and Mexico.
2. The political fight over NAFTA was unusual because many of the politicians crossed party lines and took the same side.
3. Answers will vary.

Page 91: Identifying Fact and Opinion/Genre
1. Answers will vary.
2. Answers will vary.
3. You might find this selection about NAFTA in a newsmagazine, because it is meant to inform the reader.

A Tarantula—Big Hairy Deal

Page 96: Questions
1. Tarantulas got their name from a large spider found near Taranto, Italy.
2. A tarantula finds food by picking up vibrations made by its prey as it moves.
3. A Pepsis wasp will act aggressively toward a tarantula and will try to sting it.

4. The three ways a tarantula can defend itself are through a loud hissing sound, by shedding off its hair, and finally by using its huge fangs.

Page 96: Identifying Genre and Style Techniques/Recognizing Author's Effect and Intention/Applying Passage Elements

1. This selection would more likely appear in a general-interest magazine. Answers will vary.

2. Answers will vary.

3. Answers will vary.

4. Tarantulas don't live in Antarctica because they live in warm climates.

5. People think that tarantulas make good pets because tarantulas are quiet, don't eat a lot, don't smell, make a mess, or take up much room.

Strange Case of Dr. Jekyll and Mr. Hyde

Page 115: Questions

1. Dr. Jekyll's will left everything he owned to Mr. Hyde. This bothered his lawyer because Mr. Hyde didn't seem trustworthy and he had a detestable personality.

2. Edward Hyde disappeared after the murder of Sir Danvers Carew.

3. After the murder of Carew, Dr. Jekyll began a new life of entertaining old friends, going to church, and doing good works.

4. Answers will vary.

5. Mr. Utterson and Poole found Edward Hyde lying dead on the floor when they broke into the lab.

6. Edward Hyde died after drinking a deadly potion.

7. Dr. Jekyll's mind changed from good to evil.

8. Answers will vary.

9. Answers will vary.

10. Answers will vary.